Contents

The massive size, lofty design and durable construction of churches speak of a God who is beyond us, but dwells in our midst.

Introduction

Signs and symbols dominate human lives. They dominate our secular worlds, our everyday experiences at home, work, and play. They also dominate our sacred worlds, those spiritual occasions when we pray, meditate, or worship.

A large exit sign on a freeway announces a nearby off-ramp and indicates its destinations. Large stick figures on a wall in an airport point out restrooms for men and women. The sound of a siren warns that an emergency vehicle approaches. Parents teach children to fold their hands in prayer. Catholics often begin a period of private meditation with the sign of the cross. Sounds from a church bell tower summon people inside for worship.

A *sign* is an object, a word, or an action which points to something else, leads us to knowledge of a world beyond, or communicates understanding about a reality hidden from us.

Many, perhaps most, signs are artificial. We make them up. As intelligent beings we give added meaning to words, objects, or actions. "Buckle up," a one-way-street arrow, and the policeman's raised arm convey a bit of information or knowledge beyond what we immediately perceive with our senses. Only humans, however, catch the "beyond" meaning of such artificial signs. A dog, for example, might stop momentarily before a red or green traffic light but would not understand the further message communicated.

Some signs, on the other hand, are natural; they automatically convey the added meaning by their very nature. The smoke or vapor rising from a car hood warns of heat or fire beneath it; buds on trees, new green grass, and flowers pushing out of the earth tell us spring is here; the smell of steak on a distant charcoal grill

1

evokes a clear picture of a reality we cannot see. A dog, in this last instance, would probably stay away from the fire or draw nearer to the broiling steak, grasping naturally the meaning of those signs.

A *symbol* is a unique type of sign. A symbol as a sign necessarily points to and communicates a reality more than that which our senses immediately perceive. A symbol, however, is a special kind of sign with further, deeper meanings. Symbols possess a mysterious power to evoke conscious and unconscious thoughts and feelings within us. Those ideas and emotions have a connection with and are triggered by the symbols, but go much beyond them.

For example, gold bands on a couple's fingers signify or are signs, developed by society, which indicate that they are married, are husband and wife. But such nuptial rings, as symbols, contain in addition a rich and powerful ability to stir the inner self.

Thus on certain occasions the ring may bring back memories for the couple of a special shared moment in the past; on another occasion, it may make very real to one of them the current greatness of their love; on still another, it may stimulate thoughts of peace and reassurance as it speaks of the other's commitment forever regardless of the daily ups and downs surrounding their life together.

Symbols, as the wedding band example demonstrates, possess a past, present, and future dimension. They also contain many layers of meaning and harbor that hidden power able to generate within us conscious and unconscious responses.

To visit a Roman Catholic church is to approach and enter a structure rich in signs and symbols. The very building, often massive in size, is itself a sign and a symbol of the beyond or the transcendent. For decades or centuries, up until recent times, the loftiness of the church building, its peak, spires, and crosses, combined with its solid foundation in the earth, silently spoke in every city, town, and village of the God who is above and beyond us, but still in our midst and close to us. It quietly, but strongly, says to those passing by that God is not only out there, but everywhere, all powerful, yet deeply compassionate; God not only dwells in the heavens, but walks among us. Inside a Catholic church are countless signs and symbols, some small and some very large, but all of which point to something more.

But both the outside structure and the interior elements are also part of a wider, universal reality. One will find in Catholic churches throughout the world nearly identical or at least similar signs and symbols.

Ultimately both those exterior and interior signs and symbols are meant to trigger spiritual responses within us. They can lift up our souls and transport us toward the awesome God, distant and incomprehensible, yet immanent and compassionate.

This small book endeavors to show, in word and picture, the mystery of the Catholic faith through the "things" we see in every church.

Saints

The signs and symbols inside a Catholic church are essentially but things, only material objects, even though invested with a mysterious power to lead us beyond. Moreover, those sacred items, from the holy water receptacles to the baptismal font, from the reconciliation chapels to the central altar, need people to make them come alive and fulfill their ultimate function.

In parallel fashion, some of those things or objects, for example, stained glass windows, ornate murals, and statues of saints, remind viewers of past persons who in various heroic ways walked closely with God during their lives on earth. These heroes and heroines are human models who can inspire us and heavenly helpers who intercede there on our behalf.

Two massive cathedrals, an older one on the East coast and a new one on the West coast, use artistic representations of saints to touch the hearts of those who gaze upon them. Both reflect a current trend in the Catholic Church to honor a variety of saints from every age and every place and not limit the ones honored to the ancient world or to European nations.

St. Patrick's Cathedral in New York City, located on famous Fifth Avenue and near Rockefeller Center, attracts millions of visitors each year. A stained glass window in the center of the church carries this dedication: "1879 From James Renwich, Architect." While the building is thus more than a century old, the huge bronze front doors obviously are of more recent construction.

Standing on the steps of this cathedral, visitors see at the top of these doors Christ with six apostles on either side. Below, enclosed in small squares, are these older and modern saints: St. Joseph, patron of the Church; St. Patrick, patron of this church; St. Isaac Jogues, first priest in New York; St. Frances X. Cabrini, mother of the immigrant; Ven. Kateri Tekakwitha, Lily of the Mohawks; St. Elizabeth Seton, daughter of New York.

Inside the cathedral, along each side aisle, there are chapels which have been turned into devotional shrines. Two of quite contemporary design feature St. John Neumann and St. Elizabeth Ann Seton, both of whom had strong connections to New York and both of whom died in the nineteenth century. The interior honors Mary, the mother of Jesus, with a spacious Our Lady's Chapel in the apse of the cathedral behind the main altar and, now, with a large image of Our Lady of Guadalupe at a devotional shrine off to the side of the central sanctuary.

Across the continent, in the heart of Los Angeles, stands the newly constructed and imposing Cathedral of Our Lady of the Angels, consecrated in 2002. Located on the edge of the busy Hollywood Freeway, a sixty-foot cross in the complex is visible for miles and lighted from within at night. Built in a unique way to withstand severe earthquakes, the 132-foot-high cathedral, like its counterpart in New York, greets visitors with great bronze doors. Above the entrance, Our Lady, the mother of God and mother of all peoples, welcomes those who approach. Her face reflects features of every race, and designs on the doors themselves portray symbols indigenous to diverse cultures.

St. Patrick's Cathedral, New York City

Our Lady of the Angels Cathedral, Los Angeles

There is a special shrine dedicated to Our Lady of Guadalupe, and a large image of her is visible to the millions of motorists who pass by the cathedral.

Instead of statues representing saints, the Los Angeles cathedral contains 25 tapestries which honor 133 persons, holy individuals from all races, all ages, all continents, and many occupations and vocations. A booklet for short tours calls them holy people who are "models of goodness, our ancestors in the Faith and our friends in heaven."

In both cathedrals and in Catholic churches throughout the nation, these images, whether through windows or statues, carved figures or wall murals, are signs and symbols pointing to something, in these cases, someone beyond. They recreate or represent saintly persons who both inspire and help us. But these saints, too, are signs and symbols directing us to virtues which they practiced and which we strive to imitate.

At the end of chapters in this book under the heading "Heroes and Heroines, Models and Helpers," I have sketched the lives of saints, honored in those two cathedrals, drawing out from them particular virtues worthy of our imitation.

This theology of saints as models and helpers for individuals has also led to the centuries-old practice of designating a saint as the patron or patroness of each Catholic parish or church itself. Ask any Catholic of a certain age where he or she was raised and the answer may well be "St. Andrew's" or "St. Catherine's" or "All Saints."

The primary saint or holy person, of course, is Jesus Christ. So his name or a mystery of his life on earth often finds its way into the title of a Roman Catholic parish; thus we will discover in the United States churches named Christ the King, the Holy Name of Jesus, or Transfiguration.

As we would expect, in similar fashion, many Catholics select Mary or one of the events connected with her or an invocation honoring the mother of Jesus as their model and helper, for example, Church of the Annunciation, Queen of Martyrs, Church of the Assumption.

The practice remains the same. Believers call upon these heroes and heroines to be models and helpers for the entire parish as well as for each individual within it.

I hope that this book about signs, symbols, and images of saints inside a Catholic church will assist readers in their ongoing journey to the divine, in our common call to become holy.

Chapter 1

A Warm Welcome

Charles Trueheart, an Episcopalian, fascinated by the rapid emergence of megachurches in the United States, spent one year traveling across the country to study these giant, full-service faith communities. He visited, among others, the famous Willow Grove Church of the Open Door near Chicago, Mariner's Church at Newport Beach in California, and the Fellowship of Las Colinas in Irving, Texas. Afterward he combined the results of this research into an extensive article, "Welcome to the Next Church," which appeared in the August 1966 issue of *The Atlantic Monthly*.

Trueheart discovered, surprisingly, similar ingredients or phenomena in these quite different megachurches. They included ample parking, clear signage, attractive landscaping, clean bathrooms, and cordial greeters. He also found in all of them a warm, but respectful and non-intrusive, welcoming attitude.

Any visitor to a Roman Catholic church ideally will experience those same elements which help create a warm and welcoming atmosphere. Unfortunately, because of physical limitations this will not always be the case. Many of our parishes were established and the church buildings constructed years ago, often in developed neighborhoods and at a time when the need of parking for cars was minimal or non-existent. With the passage of time, however, these areas often changed. Space was at a premium, and driving to church became the norm. Developing ample parking lots was not a practical possibility.

For example, at a national meeting for cathedral rectors or pastors, the group leader posed this question: "For how many of you is parking a major challenge?" The vast majority of the several hundred present instantly raised their hands.

The history of our own cathedral, located in the heart of Syracuse, is a case in point. The nave of the one-hundred-foot-tall church took from 1870 to 1910 to complete; its rounded sanctuary was added in the 1920s. People could walk to church from the nearby neighborhood, and those few with vehicles easily found parking spots for them during the service.

Today, not many live near the church; office buildings fill this center city area; the parish parking lot can accommodate only a handful of cars. Early birds coming for worship take the first available spots on the street near the cathedral. Latecomers squeeze into parking spaces farther and farther away from the church. When a hockey game at the neighboring arena or an opera at the auditorium coincides with a late Sunday afternoon Mass, the parking situation becomes even more troublesome.

There is little that older parishes with churches in such established neighborhoods can do to provide the desired ample parking and easy access. However, even the challenge of finding a place to park or walking some distance to the church can become a spiritual experience. We often in life outside the church face unexpected difficulties or obstacles that try our patience. In those circumstances we usually must step back, keep matters in perspective, and recover our peace. The parking/walking hassle in a sense represents the turmoil of everyday life; the serenity and quiet of a church interior parallels the necessary breaks we take to regain our perspective.

Catholic churches recently constructed in new developments present a quite different picture. Great population growths in the South and Southwest have created an obvious and desperate need there for new parishes and new churches. Practical necessity, the ideal situation, and zoning codes have subsequently combined to produce church complexes in these areas with sizeable parking lots like those in megachurches.

The newly built church of Sts. Anne and Joachim in the burgeoning southern suburb of Fargo, North Dakota, illustrates that contemporary experience. While not part of the sectional growth, for example, in Florida or Arizona, the city itself is rapidly expanding. In response to that rapid expansion, the parish has raised up on a large plot of land in the outskirts of Fargo a quite mammoth structure for worship and offices, with adequate parking available.

Making Catholic churches accessible to the handicapped represents another challenge. Some older structures were built high above ground level, with multiple steps leading up to the entrances; others, while constructed closer to the ground, still provide little adjoining space for the installation of accessible ramps. Moreover, matching the material of the ramp to the church structure can be extremely costly. For example, over twenty years ago we installed at the cathedral such a compatible ramp into the church at an expense of about $30,000. Five years ago, we completed a similar ramp to the parish office for approximately $40,000.

The same space limitations may also hinder the development of attractive landscaping, clear signage, and clean bathrooms in older Catholic churches.

Probably a majority of Catholic parishes today have developed an attitude and a process for warmly welcoming visitors. They may have official greeters at the door, name tags for newcomers, guest books to sign, gathering spaces at the entrances, refreshments after services, tours of the church, and follow-up letters to visitors.

Every Roman Catholic church ideally provides ample parking, is fully accessible, and offers a variety of services to make visitors feel comfortable and welcome. But for various reasons, as we have noted, that may not be the case. Nevertheless, even when these desirable elements are lacking, the interior riches of a Catholic church remain there to lift up the hearts of visitors.

An attractively landscaped park next to the church warmly welcomes visitors, inspires reflective prayer, and provides an accessible entrance.

Heroes and Heroines, Models and Helpers

The Spanish Connection

On December 9, 1531, Juan Diego, a fifty-seven-year-old widower living in a small village near Mexico City, made his way to a nearby barrio on a Saturday morning for a Mass honoring Mary, the mother of Jesus.

As he passed by a hill called Tepeyac, Diego heard some beautiful music, like the warbling of birds, and saw a radiant cloud within which appeared a young Native American maiden dressed like an Aztec princess. The woman spoke to him in his own language and directed that he go to the local bishop and request that a church be erected on this spot. The bishop, a native of Spain, reacted cautiously and eventually told Juan Diego to seek some sign from the lady.

Several days later, December 12, Diego's uncle was seriously ill, and Juan, trying to avoid this mysterious woman, took an alternative route seeking a priest for his ailing relative. The lady found him, however, informed Juan Diego that his uncle had been cured, and told him to pick some roses from the area as a sign for the bishop. December was not the season for roses in Mexico, and those he collected never grew in that country.

Juan Diego collected them in his cloak, or *tilma*, and carried them to the skeptical bishop. As he opened his garment, the roses fell to the ground, and the bishop knelt down before the puzzled Diego on the widower's *tilma*, where there was an image of the lady exactly as she appeared on the Tepeyac hill.

An ancient chronicle contains these words which the maiden supposedly said to Juan Diego:

> My dearest son, I am the eternal Virgin Mary, Mother of the true God . . . it is my desire that a church be built here

in this place for me, where, as your most merciful Mother
and that of all your people, I may show my loving
clemency and the compassion that I bear to the Indians,
and to those who love and seek me. . . .

After this visit with the bishop, Juan Diego learned from his
uncle that the maiden had also appeared to the seriously ill
man, healed him, and called herself "Our Lady of Guadalupe."

The bishop erected a church on that spot, and today a magnificent basilica attracts countless pilgrims who come there to
pray and recall the story of Juan Diego and Our Lady of
Guadalupe, whose feast day is celebrated on December 12.

St. Patrick's Cathedral in New York has arranged a new
shrine area containing the image of Our Lady of Guadalupe in
the front of the church near the main altar. The Cathedral of
Our Lady of the Angels in Los Angeles likewise has a shrine
honoring Mary under this title and as Patroness of the Ameri-
cas. The reverse of a twelve-foot image there honoring Our
Lady of Guadalupe is visible to motorists on the contiguous
Hollywood Freeway.

The incident of Juan Diego and Our Lady of Guadalupe has
particular significance for two reasons: (1) her appearance as an
indigenous person speaking the local language; and (2) the
honoring of people who were poor and who had suffered rather
rude and cruel treatment from some of the Spanish colonizers.

This story of St. Juan Diego and Our Lady of Guadalupe
reminds Roman Catholics of a responsibility to develop in their
hearts and actions a preferential love for the poor.

Chapter 2

Washed and Ready

The electronic carillons from the lofty bell tower of our cathedral in Syracuse tell the time of day for people in the neighborhood. They also add a joyful sound at the conclusion of weddings and a sober tolling at the end of funerals. These bells, however, also call people to worship, summoning worshipers to church a few minutes before Masses begin each weekend. Those responding to these summonses first pass through exterior doors, often of significant size, design, and weight.

In older churches they then immediately discover a vestibule, perhaps several dozen feet wide, often with another set of interior doors leading to the church proper. Within that small transition space there may be a framed announcement board indicating the times and nature of the regular services and identifying the resident clergy. Visitors will also frequently discover racks of religious literature, copies of the weekly bulletin, and various posters announcing specific events. Finally, many parishes will have ushers or greeters welcoming the worshipers and offering them assistance.

In newer or renovated churches, gathering spaces have often replaced vestibules. These larger areas generally contain the same items found in the smaller vestibules, but they facilitate people "gathering" before and particularly after the actual services. For example, during his pastorate at St. Joseph's Church in Moorhead, Minnesota, Father Donald Krebs added to the older, traditional church just such a contemporary gathering space. It connects with the church interior through a side entrance near the sanctuary. There is ample room for people to mingle. Moreover, off to the side, chairs and round tables enable parishioners to enjoy coffee and donuts afterward or even a full meal on other social occasions. Those entering the church by way of the gathering area pass by a baptismal font and can sign themselves with this holy water.

Vestibules and gathering spaces serve secular and sacred purposes. They provide a barrier or buffer between the outside world and the church interior. In winter weather and on rainy days, these serve an obviously practical purpose. At all times, however, vestibules and gathering spaces convey information and facilitate community building among those arriving for worship and those departing at the liturgy's conclusion.

However, vestibules and gathering spaces also transition people from the secular world outside to the sacred atmosphere inside a church. We normally carry a thousand concerns or preoccupations within us as we approach the church doors for a service. The semi-quiet, welcoming, and reverent area of the vestibule or gathering space can gradually and gently dissolve those busy distractions and place us in a more prayerful and contemplative mood as we move into the church proper.

Holy Water and Baptismal Fonts

The word "font" comes from the Latin word *fons, fontis,* which means fountain, spring, or source. The dictionary definition or description notes that a font is, among other things, "a basin or vessel often mounted on a pedestal in which water is contained for baptizing" or "a receptacle for holy water."

The vestibule of churches, particularly older ones, contain at least one and usually several of these holy water fonts. The basin or receptacle may be of glass, metal, some ceramic material, or even marble. They may be attached to the wall or rest upon a pedestal. Sometimes the entire pedestal and font are of one piece.

The fonts contain holy water, that is, water already blessed. Usually the blessing is done at Mass with the presiding priest praying over a container of water using one of three formulas. Form B reads as follows:

> Lord God Almighty,
> creator of all life,
> of body and soul;
> we ask you to bless this water: (the priest
>   makes a sign of the cross over the container)
> as we use it in faith,
> forgive our sins
> and save us from all illness
> and the power of evil.
> Lord,
> in your mercy
> give us living water,
> always springing up as a fountain
> of salvation:
> free us, body and soul, from every
> danger
> and admit us to your presence
> in purity of heart.
> Grant this through Christ our Lord.

Sometimes, however, a priest or deacon blesses the holy water outside of Mass. He uses the *Book of Blessings* for this task. The introduction to that blessing indicates the purpose of holy water.

> It reminds the faithful of Christ, who is given to us as the supreme divine blessing, who called himself the living water, and who in water established baptism for our sake as the sacramental sign of the blessing that brings salvation. (No. 1388)

Newer or renovated churches may have a baptismal font located at the main entrance instead of holy water receptacles. As we mentioned, that is the case at St. Joseph's in Moorhead. The baptismal font stands in the corridor linking the gathering space and the church interior. These fonts generally have spaces filled with water suitable for infant and adult immersion, but also for worshipers wishing to sign themselves as they enter the church proper.

Blessing Oneself

When Roman Catholics enter the church, they customarily bless themselves with either holy water or baptismal water. They do so by dipping the fingers of their right hand into the blessed water and then making the sign of the cross—touching forehead, chest, left shoulder, and finally right shoulder—saying quietly or thinking to themselves, "In the name of the Father, and of the Son, and of the Holy Spirit."

The *Book of Blessings* explains the significance of this symbolic gesture:

> The blessing of this water reminds us of Christ, the living water, and of the sacrament of baptism, in which we were born of water and the Holy Spirit. Whenever, therefore, we are sprinkled with this holy water or use it in blessing ourselves on entering the church or at home, we thank God for his priceless gift to us and we ask for his help to keep us faithful to the sacrament we have received in faith. (No. 1393)

Water in the Bible

The Bible in both the Old and the New Testament contains frequent references to water. That means water often occurs in Jewish and Christian teachings and practices. Here several examples from the Old Testament and the Jewish tradition:

Water creates. In the book of Genesis, the first and second stories of creation emphasize the central importance of water in God's action of creating the heavens and the earth (Genesis 1-2).

Water cleanses. When our ancestors failed to keep the divine law, God instructed Noah to build an ark and assemble in it representative animals together with himself, his wife, his sons, and their wives. Then the waters of the flood came upon the earth and a heavy rain poured down for forty days and forty nights. Every living thing on the earth was wiped out except for those in the ark. God cleansed the earth of wickedness. After the flood, God made a covenant with Noah and all living beings, promising a future recognizable sign of the divine presence and protection on earth. A bow in the clouds will frequently remind all of that covenant (Genesis 6-9).

Water liberates. As the Jewish people fled oppression in Egypt, they stood before the Red Sea with their enemies in pursuit. The waters miraculously parted, the chosen ones marched through and eventually entered the Promised Land, while the Egyptian soldiers perished as the waters flowed back upon the chariots and the charioteers (Exodus 13-15).

Here are several examples from the New Testament and the Christian tradition.

Marriage feast of Cana. At the beginning of his public ministry Christ, then around thirty, worked the first of his miracles during a wedding at Cana in Galilee. The hosts had run short of wine at the celebration. Jesus, at the request of his mother, responded to their need by changing six jars of water (twenty to thirty gallons) into "good" wine. As the headwaiter mentioned, often hosts serve the best wine first and an inferior vintage later. Not knowing the origin of this fine wine, he remarked to the host, "You have kept the good wine until now" (John 2). We see here, again, the creative hand of God using water for a divine purpose. The miracle not only indicated Jesus' special love for married couples, but also revealed his own glory, so much so that his followers began to believe in him.

Baptism in the Jordan. John the Baptist prepared people for the coming of the Messiah by preaching about repentance, or the need to change one's heart, be free of sin, and lead a better life. As a sign of their willingness to repent and to lead new lives, John baptized them with water, "for repentance." When Jesus approached John at the Jordan river and asked for baptism, John hesitated, indicating that he rather should be baptized by Christ. The Lord insisted, however, and by that action validated or gave his support to the ministry of John the Baptist and his cleansing baptismal ritual (Matthew 3). Later Jesus established the sacrament of baptism, different from John's ritual but with certain similarities to it.

Meeting with Nicodemus. A ruler of the Jewish people, Nicodemus, came to Christ at night and posed several religious questions to him. Jesus responded with the famous words: "Amen, amen, I say to you, no one can enter the kingdom of God without being born of water and Spirit." Christ went on to say that ". . . everyone who believes in him may have eternal life" (John 3).

The waters of baptism thus liberate people from the burdens of this life by making them members of the Christian community, filling them with the divine presence, and opening the gates of paradise, or heaven, to those who believe and are baptized.

Water in Everyday Life

We experience these same effects of water in our everyday human experiences. In earlier years, I always thought that grass that turned brown by summer heat and drought was dead and lifeless. It took me a few years to realize that several hours of a slow, gentle rainfall could quickly and almost miraculously bring the seemingly dead and inert grass back to life. Water does have a marvelous creative power.

One of the great joys in life is, after some hard and dirty work or very vigorous physical exercise, to plunge into a lake or stand under a warm shower. The water washes away the dirt and sweat, but also lifts up our spirits.

As we have noted, God in speaking to Noah promised to place in the clouds a bow as a reminder of the divine presence in our midst. For many people, Catholic or otherwise, multicolored, awesome rainbows do just that. They can free us from preoccupation with life's challenges on earth and raise our sights to a higher level. They make us more conscious of God walking beside us now and also remind us of a beautiful life to come in the hereafter.

Water, therefore, is a magnificent symbol, pointing to something else, but one based upon our human as well as our spiritual experiences.

Blessing of Baptismal Water

During the celebration of baptism, a priest or deacon blesses the water which will be used for this sacrament. The *Rite of Baptism for Children* provides three alternative formulas for that blessing, each of which mentions some items in the biblical, Jewish, and Christian traditions we have described. A sample invitation asks God "to give these children new life in abundance through water and the Holy Spirit" (No. 53).

The multiple invocations recall in various ways creation, the great flood, John's baptism in the Jordan, the water and blood flowing from Christ's side on the cross, and Jesus' commission to the disciples to go and teach all nations, baptizing them in the name of the Father and of the Son and of the Holy Spirit. All the blessings mention as gifts for those baptized "newness of life," "eternal life," "a new and spiritual birth," "new life," and "being born again by the power of the Holy Spirit."

Old and New Baptismal Fonts

The baptismal fonts in use during the life of our century-old cathedral in Syracuse illustrate in a special way the transition from an older design to a more contemporary concept. When I was assigned there as a newly ordained priest in 1956, the baptismal font stood in the rear corner of the church (actually near the main or front entrance). It was pedestal-like, with the font itself resting on a pillar of support.

Catholic customs for baptism at that time were quite different from today's practices. The sacrament was most often administered individually, rather than with several infants together. Few people attended the church ceremony, although many may have joined in the reception afterward. The baptism needed to be done within a month lest the child be deprived of this divine gift. The mother, as a consequence, seldom appeared, and the role of the godmother was judged to be very important since she held the baby in the absence of the birth mother. Baptisms were never celebrated within Mass. That small font in the back corner of our cathedral served adequately, although without distinction, the baptismal needs of the parish community at that time.

In 1960, a million-dollar renovation substantially altered the interior of the cathedral. Extensive marble in the sanctuary (wall, floors, altar, pulpit, communion railing), modern light fixtures, radiant floor heating, and elaborate decorative schemes on the wall brightened and beautified the inside of the church. Part of this project was to erect a separate space or building for baptisms, located off one of the entrances near the sanctuary. The interior of that small baptistry was a masterpiece.

Mosaics of colorful ceramic depict on one wall the risen Christ flanked by two trees bearing fruit with several birds and butterflies flying about. On the opposite wall eleven apostles (Judas had taken his life and a successor not yet chosen) in transfixed pose gaze upon Jesus and hear his commissioning words. That command, also in ceramic, appears in English over the baptistry's entrance: "Go, therefore, and make disciples of all nations, baptizing them in the name of the Father, and of the Son and of the Holy Spirit" (Matthew 28:19-20).

A small side wall compartment marked *Olea Sancta* in Latin on its door contained the consecrated holy oils for this and other sacraments. Stained glass windows, one with the design of a cross on it, provided natural illumination.

The font itself, very similar to the one it replaced, also rested on a pedestal, with the entire unit in white marble.

That new baptistry was a distinct improvement over the older one. It provided a unique, attractive, and noble space for this pivotal sacrament. But the renovation happened ten years too early; the beautiful and creative baptistry would, in but a decade, prove out of date and practically useless.

In 1969 the Church issued a totally new *Rite of Baptism for Children* based on the recommendations of the Second Vatican Council, which took place during the early part of the decade. Its general introduction and subsequent official documents included many detailed directives which radically changed the ritual for this sacrament and the font needed for its celebration.

The water should be clean, if possible heated beforehand, blessed at each baptism and could even be flowing as a sign of new, fresh life. Immersion was declared to be "more suitable" because it better symbolizes participation in the death and resurrection of Christ. Nevertheless, the rite of infusion (pouring water over the head of the child) might still be used.

The baptistry must be attractive, in a place easily seen by the faithful and large enough to accommodate a good number of people. Apart from the Easter season, the Easter, or paschal, candle should be placed in the baptistry or near the baptismal font so candles for each child can be lighted from it.

As far as possible, all newly born babies should be baptized at a common celebration on the same day.

Baptisms may be celebrated on any day, but Sundays are particularly suitable because of the connection that sacrament has with the death and resurrection of Christ.

The people of God (represented not only by the parents, godparents, and relatives, but also by friends, neighbors, and some members of the local church) should actually participate. If at all feasible, the mother should be present for the baptism and the celebration itself be done "within the first weeks after birth" (note the general guidance as opposed to the one month restriction). Baptisms may be celebrated even during Sunday Mass, but "this should not be done too often."

These regulations about combining baptisms, celebrating them on Sundays if possible, and with a maximum number of people present remind all that this sacrament is not an isolated individual event, but a welcoming of the child into a faith community, the body of Catholic Christians. The baptized will be supported in their spiritual journey by these people and eventually will be called upon to support others in their own journeys.

A directive about the mother being present points to the role of both parents as the prime teachers of their children in the ways of the faith.

Finally, baptism within Mass symbolizes not only the welcoming of the Christian community notion, but also the connection of baptism with the Eucharist. Baptism is the beginning of a spiritual journey meant to lead to and find its culmination in Holy Communion, the Eucharist.

In the late 1980s our cathedral underwent yet another major renovation of its interior. These changes were not merely cosmetic, designed to improve the beauty of the building, but almost totally functional, responding to the new liturgical directives.

The location and design of a new and substantive stone baptismal font reflected the many official directives. It now rests several feet to the side of the main altar, is easily accessible for baptism within Mass, and in clear view of the people, with sufficient space to enable a good number of people to observe closely the baptismal ritual. A mechanism underneath the font cleans, heats, and moves the water so that it flows. The font on the upper level is large enough for the immersion of infants. The overflow of water cascades down into a pool which measures four feet by four feet. People can draw blessed water from the pool for home use.

A baptismal font with clean, flowing, and heated water, near the altar or sanctuary, clearly visible to worshipers and suitable for the immersion of infants or adults.

More importantly, we can immerse adults receiving baptism, which usually happens on Holy Saturday at the Easter Vigil.

In one of our more inspiring liturgical moments, the adults kneel individually in about a foot of water while the bishop dips his cupped hands into the pool, sweeps up the water, and pours it over the heads of the candidates. These newly baptized then withdraw from the sanctuary, dry off, change clothes and return, washed and ready for Confirmation and their first Eucharist.

Washed and Ready

When people enter a Catholic church, they bring with them a certain amount of baggage—the frantic busyness of everyday life and a preoccupation with their personal concerns. A quiet vestibule or gathering space helps begin the process of leaving the busyness and preoccupation behind.

A sign of the cross, made with fingers dipped in holy water, reminds us of our need for inner repentance and confident faith in God's everlasting mercy.

Now spiritually somewhat washed and clean, we move into the church proper more ready to experience the divine presence in people, word, sacrament, and the many symbols about to be encountered. We are reminded that

God through the blessed waters of baptism recreates, cleanses and liberates us;

we receive a new life with the risen Lord through grace taking up residence within us;

we are cleansed of all sin;

we become members of the Christian community in which the truth makes us free;

we also have a well-founded hope for the future, trusting that washed through the waters of baptism and ready because of a Christian life on earth, we will find the gates of heaven open and a life of unimaginable joy awaiting us.

Heroes and Heroines, Models and Helpers

The French Connection

The Catholic Church has recognized the holiness of two persons, St. Theresa of the Child Jesus and Blessed André Bessette, both of whom have French backgrounds and both of whom struggled with poor health.

Saint Theresa of the Child Jesus, better known as the "Little Flower," was born in 1873. Though she lived only twenty-four years, nine of which were spent in a cloistered convent, she still exerted a significant impact upon Catholics around the world.

She developed her own "little way" of spirituality, an approach which concentrated on carrying out every action, even the smallest activity such as picking up a pin, with intense love. Her autobiography, *The Story of a Soul*, describes this path to holiness and became very popular during the first part of the twentieth century.

Illness plagued Theresa throughout her brief life. As a child she endured a three-month sickness filled with violent crises, lengthy delirium, and extended fainting spells. Despite being very frail, she performed hard physical tasks in the convent. The Little Flower also experienced lengthy periods of spiritual darkness, and in the last year of her life she succumbed to tuberculosis. She once hoped to be a missionary or a martyr, but then came to realize that her calling was to pray for others, to "save souls and pray for priests." Upon her deathbed in 1897, St. Theresa promised to continue helping others in heaven.

A shrine at St. Patrick's Cathedral in New York honoring the young saint from France contains the words of that wish: "*Je veux passer mon ciel à faire au bien sur la terre.*" "I wish to spend my heaven doing good on earth." Her feast is celebrated on October 1.

Blessed André Bessette was born in 1845 of a French Canadian couple near Montreal. Adopted at the age of twelve after his parents died, he struggled with sickness and frailty from birth. André worked at various jobs, including a short period in a United States factory during the Civil War.

At the age of twenty-five he sought to enter the Congregation of the Holy Cross in Montreal, but despite his recognized holiness, authorities turned him down because of his poor health. Later they relented, accepted the young man as a religious brother, and assigned him to be a porter, or door keeper, at Notre Dame College in Montreal.

It soon became apparent that he had the gift of healing others. That reputation quickly spread, and for decades he restored health to thousands by his prayers to St. Joseph, anointing people with oil, and speaking with those afflicted.

Brother André's dream of a magnificent oratory, or church, on Mount Royal was finally realized. Today visitors will observe there a great collection of canes and crutches, a testimony of people attributing their healing to his prayer and touch.

At the end of his life, Brother André needed four secretaries to answer the eighty thousand communications he received annually.

The frail young boy, once rejected because of his poor health, died at ninety-two. The Church declared him "Blessed" in 1982 and celebrates his feast on January 6. One of the tapestries at the Los Angeles cathedral features an image of Blessed Brother André Bessette.

These two saintly persons provide us with encouragement during times of sickness and inspire us also to pray for others.

Chapter 3

The Family Gathers

Parades and Processions

Americans love parades. During them we recall a heritage (St. Patrick's Day), rejoice in blessings (Fourth of July), and remember noble heroes (Memorial Day).

The United States military forces use precise, majestic, and solemn parades to review troops, change commandants, and bury comrades.

We use processions, a form of parade, for special occasions in our lives. Bridal parties walk to the altar in formal and carefully rehearsed fashion; graduates file into an auditorium accompanied by the traditional "Pomp and Circumstance" music; speakers, moderators, honored guests, and dignitaries line up in a defined order beforehand at a festal event and walk through the assembled standing crowd to the podium.

The Church employs processions in its worship for some of these same situations (e.g., weddings), but also uses them for other religious occasions. A class of first communicants enters the church two by two before Mass usually wearing special clothes for this major event in their lives. Confirmation candidates, all often sporting identical red robes, likewise process into the church prior to the Mass to celebrate that sacrament. Mourners accompany a casket on its journey in and out of the church, then on to the ceremony for burial of the deceased.

These illustrations remind us that parades and processions often fulfill a double function, one practical and one symbolic.

The practical value of a parade or procession may be simply to fulfill the need to move people or objects from one place to another. For example, graduates process from a waiting area to the stage and brides walk down the aisle from church entrance to the sanctuary space. There is another pragmatic function, however: the need for a community to express its shared inner sentiments in a group way. For example, the nation mourns an assassinated president or a city praises its World Series winning team.

The symbolic value of a parade or procession may be an add-on to its practical purpose, or it may stand alone as a symbol, sign, or reminder of another reality. The wedding or funeral processions in church obviously have pragmatic value, but the way they are executed points to such elements as love, gratitude, sorrow, hope and faith which surround these occasions.

On the other hand, the procession with the cross on Good Friday and the Easter candle on Holy Saturday are almost entirely symbolic, triggering thoughts and emotions about the crucifixion and resurrection as they apply to participants.

History of Processions at Mass

Processions in the context of regular Sunday Masses, however, have a varied career in the two-millennia history of the Church. For good reasons, there were, in effect, no processions at Mass during the first three centuries of Christianity. The Church in those days suffered through great persecutions. It was hardly a climate fostering outward religious displays. Moreover, because of civil restrictions, there were few Christian churches at that time. Catholics instead usually gathered for Mass in houses, catacombs, or relatively safe secret places, locations obviously not suitable for processions. Finally, the early followers of Christ were a static "waiting" people of God—they expected the Lord to return momentarily in his great Second Coming.

With the Edict of Constantine at the beginning of the fourth century, the situation completely changed. The Church now enjoyed the support, not the opposition, of the imperial government. Buildings designed for worship—churches, basilicas, and cathedrals—began to emerge in which processions were both practically necessary and symbolically rich. In addition, Christians, coming to the realization that apparently the Lord's return was not that imminent, shifted from being a "waiting" people of God. They became instead a people "on the move," a pilgrim group, a group of believers on a journey to the heavenly kingdom. Liturgical processions at Mass mirrored that shift and reinforced this new attitude.

The structure of those magnificent church buildings which began to rise at Rome starting in the fourth century reflects this development of processions. The vesting area for the numerous clergy taking part in the liturgical celebration was located near the entrance of the church at the opposite end from the apse or sanctuary. This location facilitated the lengthy and necessary procession of clergy from the entrance to the altar.

That practice continued for over a thousand years. For diverse and complex reasons, however, these major processions accompanied by music began to disappear in the last part of the second millennium. As a consequence, church structures likewise began to take a different shape. For example, most churches during the 1950s had vesting areas behind or at the side of the apse, sanctuary, or altar. Consequently, the priest needed to walk only a few steps from the sacristy or vesting area to the altar and sanctuary. There was seldom any singing during this abbreviated opening procession; instead, the server often rang a bell announcing the priest's entrance, and the people rose in silence to greet him.

In the second half of the twentieth century, Church leaders through official documents sought to resurrect the various processions at Mass and recover their spiritual richness. Processions occurred at the Entrance, the Gospel, the Presentation of Gifts (Offertory), Communion, and at the end of the liturgy.

Church structures changed accordingly. New churches and renovated older structures placed the vestry area near the main entrance, again with only a smaller area for altar supplies near the sanctuary. Masses now begin with a procession of clergy and liturgical ministers accompanied by congregational singing moving from this vesting space down the main aisle to the altar; there is a similar recessional at the end. Smaller, basically functional processions, but with symbolic meaning, occur at the Gospel, Presentation of Gifts, and Communion rites.

These processions with music accompaniment help to gather into a believing community the assembled worshipers, aware that they are a pilgrim people of God making their way on an unpredictable journey to eternal life and the kingdom of heaven.

Cross and Crucifix

Usually an altar server bearing a tall processional cross leads the major liturgical ministers from the main entrance through the congregation to the altar.

The *cross*, of course, is the dominant symbol of Christianity. It was on a cross at Calvary that Jesus died for us; it was upon this tree of life that Christ shed his precious blood and obtained our salvation; it was a way of the cross that the Savior predicted would be the path Christians must follow.

Often a cross at the pinnacle of a church roof identifies this as a Christian place of worship. Men and women wear necklaces with small crosses suspended from them. Religious books, including Bibles, frequently have a cross stamped upon their covers.

Making a sign of the cross is, as we mentioned earlier, a distinctive Roman Catholic symbol. Mass begins and ends with this gesture. Grace before meals is usually preceded by a sign of the cross. Baseball players often sign themselves when stepping up to the plate, and foul shooters do the same in a basketball game. That

A large crucifix, with the figure of Christ fastened to the cross, is on or near the altar in the sanctuary, sometimes as a permanent fixture and sometimes as a processional cross, sometimes plain and sometimes decorated.

gesture not only recalls Good Friday and the crucifixion, it also reflects faith in one God, in the Holy Trinity—Father, Son and Holy Spirit, and three divine persons in the one God. Moreover, it implies a belief in the Son's coming into the world and his rising from the tomb.

Many associate a particular form of the cross, the *crucifix*, with Roman Catholics. The word means, in its Latin roots, fixed to the cross. Thus a figure of Christ is attached to the cross. In Eastern churches there is often a painting of Jesus on the cross; in the Western churches it more customarily is a sculptured figure of Christ fixed to the intersecting beams.

During the Middle Ages the crucifix began to dominate over the simple cross. The crucifix then sometimes depicted Jesus vested in the robes of a king or priest, or with a crown of jewels placed on the Savior's head. In the thirteenth century, Church preaching and teaching concentrated on the sufferings of Jesus, and with that emphasis the representations of the crucified Lord became more starkly realistic.

In was only in 1570, however, with the *Roman Missal* of Pius V, that the Church imposed an obligation to have a crucifix on the altar, a requirement which meant a cross should be on, above, or beside the altar. Ideally the cross or crucifix would be large enough for the entire congregation to see it quite clearly.

During the last half of the twentieth century there was a movement to return to the plain cross or to display a risen Christ instead of a suffering Savior on the crucifix. That trend seems to have subsided. Current regulations direct that a cross, with the figure of Christ crucified upon it, be positioned either on or near the altar and be clearly visible to the people gathered for worship.

Normally there will be only one dominant crucifix in a church. At the end of the journey to the altar, the server usually places the processional cross or crucifix in a base near the altar facing the people, waiting for its use in the recessional at the completion of Mass.

Candles

At major family meals, solemn banquets, or even dinners at fine restaurants, candles add to the festal nature of the occasion. We also use scented candles to create an intimate atmosphere for small house parties; brides envision candlelight weddings; great crowds hold small candles during civic services like those remembering the Trade Center tragedies of September 11, 2001.

A little later, but still relatively early in its history, around the middle of the first millennium, the church began to use candles for eucharistic services. There may have been some functional purposes for this addition—illumination and warmth. But more likely the dominant reasons were symbolic in nature.

The use of candles for solemnity and festiveness, as in the secular settings we have mentioned, would, of course, apply to the sacred world of worship. The Church, however, could cite many other symbolic connections between flickering candles and the Catholic faith.

- The concept of light conquering darkness is a recurrent theme in both the Hebrew Scriptures and the Christian Bible.
- Jesus Christ is the true light of the world, a beacon shining in the midst of darkness.
- The Mass is a sacred banquet and a holy meal taking place on a consecrated altar considered to be the table of the Lord.
- Pure beeswax, for years the standard component of church candles, speaks to the purity of God, Jesus, and the ritual being celebrated.
- Candles burn themselves out, a reminder of the self-giving action of Christ on the cross and of the unselfish love for others expected of Christians.

- The use of candles creates an aura of reverence, a sense of wonder, an attitude of respect for the sacred ritual taking place.

In the entrance journey to the altar, two servers, each carrying a lighted candle, walk on either side of the server bearing the processional cross. Having reached the front of the church, servers place the candles on or around the altar in a way dictated by the design of the altar and the sanctuary.

It is an interesting historical fact that the custom of having two candles for an ordinary Mass, six for a solemn function, and seven when a bishop presides dates back to the twelfth century. The Church continues that specific tradition today. Its latest directives for the Mass require at least two lighted candles for every celebration, four or six for a Sunday or holiday Mass, and seven if the bishop of the diocese presides.

In recent years, for practical purposes, some churches have begun to use oil instead of beeswax as the main ingredient of the altar candles.

The Easter Candle

A tall, massive candle stands in the sanctuary or near the baptismal font. Called the Easter, Passover, or paschal candle, it is a key element in perhaps the most important liturgical celebration of the year, the Easter Vigil Mass on Holy Saturday.

This lengthy service, usually at least two hours, dramatizes the darkness to light, death to life, motif of Christianity. All lights in the church are extinguished. At or outside the main entrance a flame is struck, blessed, and used to ignite a small fire. From that source, the Easter candle is lighted.

In many and probably most churches, however, the Easter candle has additional symbols stamped or pressed into its surface. These include (1) alpha and omega, the first and last letters of the

The substantial and tall Easter, paschal, or Passover candle is used at the Holy Saturday Vigil liturgy. It is lighted at Sunday Masses during the Easter season and at baptisms and funerals throughout the year.

Greek alphabet, signifying that God is the beginning and the end—everything; (2) the current year; as well as (3) five grains of incense covered with wax and inserted into the candle itself in the form of a cross. The presiding priest recites these words as he inserts the five grains: "By his holy and glorious wounds may Christ our Lord guard us and keep us."

With these rites completed and the candle lighted, the priest says: "May the light of Christ, rising in glory, dispel the darkness of our hearts and minds."

The Holy Saturday procession begins with a small cluster of ministers and servers moving down the aisle toward the sanctuary. Three times during that journey, the priest or deacon holds up the burning Easter candle and proclaims: "Christ our light." The congregations responds, "Thanks be to God." After the first proclamation, servers light their own tapers from the Easter candle and spread that flame to all in the church who hold small candles with protective paper shields.

When the procession arrives in the sanctuary the Easter candle is placed in a prominent position. One of the ministers then sings the famous Easter proclamation as the congregation remains standing with lighted tapers in hand. The text recalls the darkness to light, death to life, theme of the Easter event.

The Easter candle remains in the sanctuary during the Easter season (Easter to Pentecost) and is lighted for Sunday Masses throughout that period. It is also lighted for all baptisms and funerals both during Easter time and throughout the year.

Our Lady of the Angels

On September 2, 2000, Cardinal Roger M. Mahoney dedicated the extraordinary Our Lady of the Angels Cathedral in Los Angeles. For years to come this innovative religious complex, located in the midst of busy freeways, will attract countless visitors and call them to prayer.

Prior to its dedication a group enjoyed a preliminary tour of the new cathedral. They walked from the exterior plaza through a long corridor singing familiar hymns. Turning right at the end they entered the main space and suddenly stopped singing. The visitors were stunned by the worship area, in awe of it, and just wanted to look at this marvelous creation.

In similar, although less dramatic fashion, visitors to Catholic churches pass through a transitional entrance area and move into the worship space proper. They, too, may stop, be stunned by the beauty and prayerfulness of the building's interior, and find themselves quietly transported into another world, lifted to a transcendent level, experiencing the God who is beyond, but still close to us. If they remain for Mass they will also recognize that those who gather for worship are a pilgrim people on the move, at once striving for that transcendent goal, but also building a community of believers who care deeply about each other and others, especially those in need.

Heroes and Heroines, Models and Helpers

The Czech and German Connection

Visitors entering St. Patrick's Cathedral in New York City will notice along the left side facing the altar a series of alcoves with statues of saints in them. Most reflect the century-old character of this church, but one of these shrines is of a much brighter and newer construction. It contains an image of St. John Neumann with some children listening to him. He was canonized a saint in recent times—1977—by Pope Paul VI.

The tapestries at the Cathedral of Our Lady of Angels in Los Angeles also includes among its 133 holy persons a representation of St. John Neumann. Who is this man, now a saint of the Catholic Church?

Born on March 28, 1811, in what is now the Czech Republic, he followed a dream, came to the United States, and was ordained a priest in New York City at the age of twenty-five. For a number of years he traveled throughout New York State as a missionary, spending long hours in solitude and silence during these journeys from place to place. Later he joined the Redemptorist religious community, continued his missionary work, although now laboring in Maryland, Pennsylvania, Ohio, and the American frontier.

Father Neumann, an accomplished linguist who spoke twelve languages, composed in German two catechisms and a Bible history for the people he served.

Eventually he was named bishop of Philadelphia, and there he quickly established an extensive Catholic school system, which continues today.

Despite his organizing skills and talent for administration, Bishop Neumann was known more for his personal holiness and deep prayer life. Immediately after his death in 1860, crowds flocked to his grave, recognizing the goodness of the man and asking for his help in heaven.

St. John Neumann reminds us that to keep close to God in the midst of our busy lives, we need to have some time set aside for quiet prayer each day.

The Church celebrates his feast on January 5.

Part II

The Voice of God

Chapter 4

A Holy Place

Two sections in early chapters of the Acts of the Apostles provide an idealistic description of life in the Christian Church during the first century. The followers of Christ were of one mind and heart, shared things in common, and made sure that there were no needy persons among them. They powerfully brought the message of Jesus to others with their words, which were accompanied by marvelous signs and wonders.

But every day they gathered in the temple to pray and hear God's word, then broke bread in their homes. There was great joy among them; they praised God unceasingly; many outside their community were so touched that they became Christians (Acts 2 and 4).

Note that there was a vertical and a horizontal dimension to their lives. They were close to one another and shared things in common. They formed a community of caring people—the horizontal feature of their lives. But they also assembled for worship, praising God and listening to God's words for them—the vertical aspect of their lives.

Catholics strive to imitate that ideal Christian Church—a gathering of strong believers who care for one another and others, but who also worship a transcendent God and listen to the Creator's holy words for them. The church's exterior structure and interior furnishings have been designed to foster those horizontal and vertical dimensions of Christian life.

A Church's Structure

The first Christians called their place of worship the *domus Dei*, the house of God, or even the Lord's house. Our English word "church" derives from a Latin word which means the assembly, a calling together of people for prayer. Those ancient Christians termed a large or principal church a basilica, or house of the king.

Two of the first basilicas, St. John Lateran and St. Peter's, both in Rome and both constructed in the fourth century, reflect the way Christians worshiped then and would continue to do so for centuries. The bishop's or priest's chair is in the center of the apse behind the altar. The altar, free standing, is nearer the congregation and enables the presiding clergy to face the people during Mass. The people, of course, face the priest and the altar. Visitors to those basilicas will recognize that that structure basically remains the same now, 1,700 years later. In this arrangement the priest and people face one another, easily exchange words with each other, and together praise God as a community.

For various complex historical and theological reasons, a shift took place in the late Middle Ages. With a tabernacle containing the reserved eucharistic Christ fixed to the center of the altar, the priest now celebrated Mass facing the tabernacle and wall with his back to the people. He would turn to them for greetings and blessings. The Mass usually was in Latin with minimal active participation by the people in the pews and little or no congregational singing.

This arrangement tended to stress the vertical and diminish the horizontal dimension of worship at Mass; it heightened an individualistic rather than a communal approach to the liturgy. Some viewed this development of the priest and people facing in the same direction praising God as signifying their union with the priest as their leader. Many judged these for the most part silent or quiet Masses quite positively, as reverent, sacred, and filled with a sense of mystery, transcendence, and awe.

In the middle of the twentieth century, there was a movement to restore the ancient notion of Mass "facing the people." This effort sought to maintain the desirable vertical aspect of prayer-fulness, reverence, and the sacred while enhancing the horizontal dimension of community participation by all in the Mass ritual. That, of course, required a shift in the location of both the altar and the tabernacle. In this new arrangement, the tabernacle was removed from the altar to another place of prominence, and the altar moved from the rear of the sanctuary to a place nearer the people.

The transformation received official sanction, as reflected in the new *Roman Missal* of 1970, which was further revised in 2000. Its directives for the sanctuary declare that there should be a fixed, dedicated freestanding altar, allowing ministers easily to walk around it and facilitating Mass celebrated facing the people, "which is desirable whenever possible" (No. 299). Newly con-structed churches have been designed to comply with this direc-tive. Older churches usually have retained their older altars nearer the back wall of the apse, but have added a new altar suitable for Mass facing the people at the opposite end of the sanctuary toward the congregation.

Pews and Chairs

When the opening procession moves from the main entrance to the sanctuary, it passes through the assembled people, who usu-ally are located in fixed pews, but sometimes in rows of chairs. The pews generally are of finished wood, although occasionally parishes upholster the pews or provide detachable cushions for more comfortable seating during the readings and homily.

There was an impetus during the second half of the twentieth century to install chairs instead of pews in churches to provide greater flexibility of movement and to offer the possibility of re-arranging the seating for different functions. Although such chairs with or without kneelers continue to be somewhat popular in small chapels, the trend to replace pews with them never seemed to gain momentum.

Pews with kneelers which can be raised or lowered (for standing or kneeling during the service) remain probably the most common feature in the nave of Catholic churches throughout the United States. They facilitate the different postures traditional at Catholic Masses—kneeling, standing, or sitting. Raising the kneelers makes it much easier for those present to stand at appropriate times, to leave the pews for Communion, to return to the pews after receiving Communion, and to depart at the end.

Kneeling can express our inner sense of repentance or unworthiness, but it also communicates our attitude of awe and adoration in the presence of the divine. We see a parallel to this latter sentiment in the rather similar gesture among Muslims, who bow with foreheads to the ground several times each day as they praise God, or Allah.

Standing indicates our respect or attentiveness. Catholics at Mass stand for certain prayers, during the proclamation of the Gospel, and throughout the processional or recessional.

We respond in the same fashion or for the same reason in our lives outside of church. For example, reporters stand when the president enters the room for a media conference, and we rise at public functions for the pledge of allegiance.

Sitting reflects an attitude of receptiveness, of attentiveness to the message we are about to hear. Whether the holy words are from pages of the Bible or the lips of the preacher/homilist we sit ready and willing to listen with open ears, minds, and hearts.

The Sanctuary Arrangement

The renovation of our cathedral in Syracuse in 1960 reflects the sanctuary arrangement common in the United States during the first half of the twentieth century. The massive white marble altar was at the rear of the sanctuary, almost touching the back wall. On the altar but even nearer the wall were a large bronze tabernacle, a huge crucifix, and seven very tall and substantial candleholders. The pulpit, also of white marble and significant in size, was at the edge of the sanctuary in front of the first pews. A curved marble communion railing with bronze decorations matching the altar furnishings separated the pews, or nave, from the sanctuary, or apse.

We can discover vestiges of this arrangement in older churches both here and abroad. Often a very large pulpit dominated the worship area, even being located in the middle of the nave.

That arrangement focused upon the presence of the Lord in the tabernacle, the preaching from the pulpit, and the sacrifice at the altar.

Directives from the revised missal of 1970 altered this arrangement. The tabernacle was transferred to another place of prominence, which we will discuss later, and the communion railing was removed. The sanctuary now had three focal points: the chair for the presiding priest, the ambo (formerly the pulpit, a location for readings and preaching), and the altar facing the people. These were to be arranged and designed to give a sense of unity and integration to the Mass ritual itself.

Previously, Offertory, Consecration, and Communion were the key words describing the essential elements of the Mass. The Church required that for Catholics to fulfill the obligation of attending Sunday Mass they must, at a minimum, be present for these three indispensable parts. Missing the opening prayers, readings, or concluding prayers was unacceptable, but a much less serious offense.

After 1970 the Mass format became instead Introductory Rites, Liturgy of the Word, Liturgy of the Eucharist (which included Preparation of the Gifts, Eucharistic Prayer, and Communion Rite), and Concluding Rites. There was especially to be a close connection between the biblical readings and the eucharistic prayer, between the ambo and the altar.

The arrangement of the sanctuary often reflects this integration. Some churches have two candles on either side of the ambo; others move the candles from the ambo after the Liturgy of the Word to the altar for the Liturgy of the Eucharist. Even the style, color, or decoration of ambo and altar are sometimes similar or identical.

The Mass ritual likewise reflects the link between the two. A directive indicates that the preacher should *not* begin or conclude his words with a traditional sign of the cross. That separates the content of the words being preached from the biblical texts just proclaimed. Moreover, the appropriate term is no longer a sermon, but a homily, and it should draw its inspiration from ideas in the scriptural readings, the texts of the Mass, or the mystery being celebrated and apply them to the contemporary situation.

The emphasis now is on word and sacrament.

The elimination of the railing reflected not only different ways for the congregation to receive Holy Communion but also a closer bond or communion between presiding priest and the assembled faithful.

Sacred Windows

In a remarkable book, *Heaven in Stone and Glass* (New York: Crossroad, 2000), Chicago professor Father Robert Barron maintains that the Gothic cathedrals such as Notre Dame in Paris or Chartres, also in France, "teach the faith and focus the journey of the Spirit." They do so, he argues, by their very unique external structure, but also by such other elements as their towers, naves, and windows. Those magnificent stained glass windows, some portraying saintly figures of the past and others featuring symbolic religious designs, teach and inspire. They communicate truths of the Catholic faith, but also lift up hearts to another world.

In our contemporary society with so many persons, especially younger people, religiously illiterate, these windows can be great

Stained glass windows depicting past saintly persons or spiritual events both inspire and instruct.

teaching tools. They also can provide to those who yearn for the spiritual in our very secularized world an experience of the sacred here on earth.

The stained glass windows of our century-old Gothic cathedral illustrate the style of windows in many of the Catholic churches built throughout the United States before the mid-point of the twentieth century. We have handwritten correspondence dating back to the late 1800s between the Irish rector of the cathedral and the Mayer Company in Munich, Germany. He outlined his desires for the type of stained glass windows, and they negotiated the price—about $13,000. A century later the restoration of these windows and our three-thousand-pipe organ cost over $600,000—an interesting indication of inflation over the years.

A large rose window in the front wall of the church greets visitors as they enter the building and, more, inspires them as they leave. Like rose windows in the famous European cathedrals, it is circular, a symbol of wholeness, completeness, and infinity. Eight smaller circles, each depicting an angel, surround the main circular scene. Seven in sacred symbolism is considered the completion of time; eight thus speaks beyond time, or eternity.

In the larger circle the Virgin Mary kneels and is receiving a crown (Queen of Heaven and Earth) from Christ who wears his own crown as King of Kings and Lord of Lords. God the Father is represented as an older man with a long beard (today some would object to that image) and God the Holy Spirit as a dove.

Interior lights illumine this quite beautiful window on the outside at night for those walking or driving by the plaza in front of the church.

On either side of the nave, sixteen windows portray figures from both the Jewish and Christian traditions. Along one wall we meet eight familiar persons, including Abraham and Solomon, Moses and Aaron. Symbolic items are linked to each individual— Moses with the two tablets of the Ten Commandments and Solomon with a plan of the temple. The windows continue with four Jewish prophets—Ezekiel, Elijah, Jeremiah, and Daniel—and the four Christian evangelists—Matthew, Mark, Luke, and John. Along the opposite side wall, we meet the twelve apostles and four early doctors and saints of the Church—Gregory the Great, Ambrose, Augustine, and Jerome.

High above is a collection of later, more contemporary saints (remember that the original construction was completed around 1900). These include St. Francis of Assisi and St. Clare, St. Catherine of Siena and St. Dominic.

The apse was completed later. Five large stained glass windows decorate the curved apse wall. They depict the annunciation, nativity, Immaculate Conception (the title of the cathedral), crucifixion, and resurrection.

Various other stained glass windows throughout the church further contribute to the beauty of the interior.

We conduct many tours of the cathedral, most often a class of confirmation candidates and their guides or youth groups from parishes of the diocese. Explaining these various windows to those young people (and their adult companions) always exemplifies to me how powerful a teaching tool they are.

We also celebrate over seventy-five weddings annually at the cathedral. Many select this church because of its size, traditional structure, and beauty. The stained glass windows, of course, contribute significantly to that attractiveness.

During the second half of the twentieth century, there was a shift away from stained glass windows, or at least from the kind of representations seen in our cathedral. Clear windows or stained glass panes, but with only straight color or symbolic designs, became more common. My guess is that there may be now a revitalization of interest in the older style of stained glass windows.

When visitors first enter our cathedral, they often are almost speechless as they gaze around the interior, at the one-hundred-foot ceiling, the large sanctuary, and the stained glass windows. "What a beautiful church," they exclaim. They intimate by their remark that it is indeed a holy place, in which they experience in a quiet, special way the presence of God.

Heroes and Heroines, Models and Helpers

The English Connection

On June 22, the Church celebrates the feast of St. Thomas More (1478-1535), an Englishman who was beheaded by the king because he refused to approve of the monarch's actions or obey his decrees.

More, made famous in modern times by the play *A Man for All Seasons,* was a scholar, a lawyer, twice married, the father of four children, a diplomat, and, eventually, the chancellor of England. He was judged to be the epitome of a gentleman, a deeply spiritual person, and an individual of great integrity.

That integrity cost him his life. For religious reasons, he would not endorse King Henry VIII's divorce from Catherine of Aragon so that the monarch might marry Anne Boleyn. Out of similar motivation, Thomas More rejected the king's decision to become supreme head of the Church of England. By that action King Henry VIII severed his connection with Rome and rejected the pope as head of the universal Church. The king accused More of treason and consigned him to the Tower of London because his former chancellor would not swear to the Act of Succession nor to the Oath of Supremacy. When Thomas More remained adamant in his refusal, the king ordered his death by beheading.

Four hundred years later, the Church declared him to be a saint, and in 2000, Pope John Paul II named him patron of political leaders. He is one of those over one hundred holy persons imaged on the tapestries of the Cathedral of Our Lady of Angels in Los Angeles.

Some years ago, John Kennedy wrote *Profiles in Courage*. St. Thomas More was not in that book, but certainly could have been. His example on earth and prayers now in heaven should help us be courageous when called to do so.

Chapter 5

Holy Words and Holy Eucharist

There are several Gospel incidents involving Jesus, his immediate followers, stormy weather, and a boat. In one, Christ is sound asleep as the turbulent waves spill into the vessel threatening to sink it. The disciples cry out, "Lord, save us, we are perishing." Jesus rises from his slumber, rebukes their lack of faith, and swiftly stills the wind and calms the sea (Mark 4:35-41). In a second episode, his followers are on the Sea of Galilee struggling with a strong storm when Christ comes to them walking on the water. After an exchange with Peter, Jesus climbs into the boat and, again, quiets both roaring gale and ugly waves (Matthew 14:22-33).

Those who enter Catholic churches usually experience something similar. They sense almost immediately an atmosphere of safety and peacefulness, of security and serenity. It is as if Jesus, present in the church, stills, calms, and quiets the inner storms we face in everyday life.

Names for the main sections of the church interior reflect these images. The center section is called the nave, apparently derived from the Latin word *navis,* which means boat or ship. The area for the chair, pulpit, and altar is called the sanctuary, derived also from a Latin word, *sanctus,* which means holy, sacred, or set aside for divine purposes. The extension of the word "sanctuary" leads us to the commonly used notion of a refuge or safe and secure haven. In the nave and within the sanctuary we encounter Christ, the powerful Savior who offers us a safe harbor in the midst of storms and fills us with a serene peace.

Presiding Chair

The sanctuary is where the priest, deacon, and other ministers exercise their functions, especially at the priest's chair. It is also the location of the ambo, at which God's holy words are proclaimed, and of the altar itself. A sanctuary should be slightly elevated and/or distinctively designed so as to set it off from the body of the church and to enable the people easily to see it.

The priest celebrant presides over the assembly and directs their prayer. His chair should stand as a symbol of that function without in any way resembling a throne. There are usually additional less prominent chairs in the sanctuary for the liturgical ministers.

The priest, standing by the chair, leads the community in prayer at the beginning, around the middle, and at the conclusion of Mass. He reads or sings prayers taken from the *Sacramentary*, a book, usually with a red cover, which contains the official prayers for all Masses. That text includes, among other formulas, a remarkable collection of some two thousand petitions for Sundays and weekdays, as well as for celebration of saints' feasts and special occasions like weddings, funerals, and civic events.

During the reciting or singing of these prayers the priest extends his hands and lifts them up in an *orans*, or praying, position. God, of course, is everywhere. Still, with our human limitations we often think of the Lord being above, "up there," beyond us. The outstretched arms consequently symbolize our prayers of pleading directed heavenward, but also our need and willingness to receive back from on high God's response to these petitions.

Ambo or Table of God's Word

With the introductory rites of the Mass completed, all present sit and prepare to hear proclaimed God's holy words.

By their location, style, and construction the presiding priest's chair, the ambo or lectern, and the altar reflect and strengthen the link between word and sacrament.

The focus turns to what once was commonly called the lectern or pulpit and is now termed the ambo. Ambo refers to the large pulpit or reading desk of early Christian and contemporary Greek and Balkan churches. During certain periods of the Church's history there were two places for the proclamation of the Scriptures—one, the epistle side (for the first reading), and the other, for the Gospel (for the Gospel text). In current thinking and practice, there is only a single ambo—an arrangement which symbolizes and stresses the oneness or link between the Old and New Testaments, or in the preferred present terminology, the Hebrew Scriptures and the Christian Scriptures.

Church directives indicate that because of the dignity of God's word the ambo should be stationary, not a movable stand; it should be a natural focal point for this part of the Mass, the Liturgy of the Word; it should be so designed, located, and furnished that everyone present can see and hear the proclaimers of the Word.

New and renovated Catholic churches usually also feature an ambo and altar with similar or identical design, color, and material that reflect the close connection between the Liturgy of the Word (ambo) and Liturgy of the Eucharist (altar). There may also be candles on either side of the ambo to stress that Christ the light of the world is speaking to us through these holy words from both the Hebrew and Christian traditions. In some instances these are not fixed, but moveable candles, capable of being transferred to the altar at the conclusion of the Liturgy of the Word. Finally, those churches will almost certainly have installed state of the art sound systems for better communication of God's word.

The Mass has always included readings from the Bible. Prior to the 1960s, however, they were limited to a one-year cycle of texts for Sundays and included a rather meager selection of scriptural passages for weekdays and other liturgical celebrations.

This changed during that decade. The Church directed scriptural scholars and liturgical experts to develop a new approach that would open up the treasures of the Bible more widely to

Christian people and foster within them a warm and living love for these holy words. The results of that prodigious effort was a magnificent milestone for Catholic worship and a positive development which has influenced other mainline Christian churches. This milestone and development was a massive lectionary of biblical readings organized for use on Sundays, weekdays, and other special occasions.

That new lectionary provides a three-year cycle of biblical readings for Sundays and solemn feasts, a two-year cycle for weekdays, and an enormous list of suitable texts for special occasions. For example, couples may select for their wedding celebration in church three readings from thirty-two Hebrew and Christian scriptural passages; families planning a funeral service have the option of choosing from nearly fifty biblical excerpts; those planning Masses in the aftermath of the September 11, 2001, event likewise found an ample supply of appropriate texts in the lectionary.

There was a lengthy and controversial process involved in translating that list of biblical readings into English texts which were both accurate versions of the original words and suitable for proclamation in church. After many delays, the compromise official translations appeared in 2002 as a four-volume series.

Once the books were issued in that format, however, publishers began to develop more elegant and readable volumes for actual worship, especially on Sundays and major occasions. These large bound volumes with distinct and dignified covers include a Book of Gospels and lectionaries for each of the three cycles (A, B, C). Those worshiping at weekend Masses would most likely see a minister holding the Book of Gospels aloft at eye level walking in the entrance procession and placing this handsome volume upright on the altar. Later the priest or deacon would carry the book, held similarly, in a procession from the altar to the ambo. After the proclamation of the Gospel, the book itself often would be placed open on a stand before the ambo.

The larger bound volume for the first two readings would normally be checked by the lectors beforehand and then placed upon the ambo open and ready for proclamation.

These lectionaries do not contain every word that occurs in the Bible. Nevertheless, if a person participated in Mass every day for three years, that person would hear a significant portion of the both the Hebrew and Christian Scriptures.

Positive Effects

The development and implementation of the new lectionary has had an enormous positive impact upon Catholic and other Christian churches.

- A large corps of lay readers or lectors take seriously this ministry of proclaiming the first two readings. They frequently have a handy annual commentary at home and study the text for understanding and better communication of the message to others.
- Those who regularly assist at weekend Masses will over a three-year period be exposed to a substantial number of biblical passages.
- People who make daily Mass part of their devotional life have the opportunity to hear a two-year cycle of additional readings, most of which do not occur during the Sunday scheme.
- Engaged couples instantly welcomed the idea of selecting readings for their nuptial service. Previous to the new lectionary, the texts (an epistle and Gospel) were always the same, and not the most felicitous ones at that. Now they could choose not only the biblical, but other texts as well. Some doubted that pastors would provide or that couples would use booklets containing these alternatives. Fortunately, these doubts were put to rest within months. In 1970 I wrote and Ave Maria Press published *Together for Life,* a small text with all the optional readings and prayers in it. Today, many print-

ings and revisions thirty years later, over nine million copies are in the hands of couples. This means that nearly two-thirds of the engaged have used this text to plan their wedding celebration, including selections of the biblical passages they prefer.

- The number of families grieving over the loss of someone they love who select their texts for a funeral liturgy has likewise grown dramatically, although not to the same extent as for engaged couples.
- Some mainline Protestant churches have adopted the revised Roman Catholic lectionary for their own Sunday worship, although with some adjustments. That has facilitated shared ecumenical homily or sermon preparation among Catholic priests and Protestant ministers.

The dream or ideal sketched by the bishops at the Second Vatican Council that the biblical treasures be opened more widely and that Roman Catholics develop a warm and living love for the scriptures has certainly been realized.

Missalettes and Hymnals

During the first half of the twentieth century, when the Mass was totally in Latin, many Catholics used small "missals" to follow the liturgy. The large book for the priest at the altar, usually totally in Latin and with a red cover, was called the *Missale Romanum,* or *Roman Missal.* Religious publishers as a consequence developed various books or booklets with translations of this text for people in the pews. A pocket-size paperback version, *My Sunday Missal,* contained the Latin text on one side and the English or vernacular version on the other. There were also sketches or pictures indicating the actions of the priest at the altar to help worshipers keep pace with the flow of the Mass. These little books frequently featured a numerical system to assist the reader in locating the variable parts of the liturgy (the changeable prayers and readings) as well as the unchanging basic order of the Mass.

Larger, hard-cover volumes entitled *The Sunday Missal* were more sturdy and included ribbons to mark the changeable and unchanging portions of the liturgical celebration. Similar daily missals provided texts, translations, and multiple ribbons for weekday Masses.

At Sunday Masses, participants watched with reverence as the sacred events unfolded at the altar (in Latin, often in silence or with subdued tone, and with most actions concealed because the priest for the most part had his back to the people as he faced the altar). They also may have recited certain devotional prayers (e.g., the rosary) or read their missals. Some even proclaimed that the best way to participate was by following the Mass prayers through the translation in these booklets or books.

Missals became a dominant part of Roman Catholic spirituality throughout the United States during that period. People read them in preparation for Mass and prayerfully followed these texts during the Eucharist. However, there was a complexity or a challenge in this procedure. The priest often could recite the Latin words faster than the person in the pew could cover the longer English translation and thus finished the Eucharist before the earnest missal reader was able to do so.

All of this changed in the 1960s. The priest at the altar began to face the people; he celebrated Mass in the vernacular languages; the assembled worshipers participated through word, song, and action.

At the same time there developed a need for permanent hymnals and a desire for disposable booklets, called missalettes, containing the Mass texts. In most Catholic churches today, visitors will note a bracket or enclosure fixed in some fashion to the pew or chair containing a missalette or hymnal or both.

Liturgical leaders and biblical scholars have debated the wisdom of including the scriptural readings in these hymnals or missalettes. The liturgical experts argue that the proclaimer of these holy texts communicates not only spoken words, but also faith and interpretation through presence and gesture. Individuals focused on the printed text miss the latter. The biblical experts argue that by reading the inspired words and at the same time listening to them they receive the message through two of our senses—sight and sound.

Moreover, scripture scholars would further maintain that inadequate sound systems, inarticulate proclaimers, and worshipers with impaired hearing make merely verbal communication of God's word difficult at best and sometimes nearly impossible. On the other hand, experience shows that superb and unique proclaimers automatically command people's attention. Teenager Peter Cantone is that kind of superb proclaimer. Similarly, no one coughs and all observe closely as Kathy O'Neill, a born-blind individual, proclaims the readings by tracing her fingers over raised Braille figures.

The Altar or Table of God's Body

The late Benedictine Father Godfrey Diekmann was a professor of theology, a distinguished leader of the liturgical renewal during the middle of the last century, and a consultant at the Second Vatican Council during the early 1960s. He often maintained that the doctrinal basis for all of the worship changes flowing from that Second Vatican Council could be found in article 7 of the "Constitution on the Sacred Liturgy."

In this section the bishops who were gathered in Rome for those deliberations stated that to achieve the desired spiritual renewal of God's people, Christ is always present in the Church, especially in her liturgical celebrations. The paragraph then lists various ways in which such a presence takes place: for example, in the sacraments, when two or three gather in Jesus' name, and in the Holy Scriptures. The paragraph specifically remarks that it is Christ himself who speaks when the Holy Scriptures are read in the church.

The bishops also point out, however, the unique presence of Jesus in the Eucharist. They remind us that Christ is present in the sacrifice of the Mass, in Holy Communion, and in the sacrament reserved for adoration prayer and for distribution to the sick.

The Mass ritual which began at the presiding priest's chair and then moved to the ambo for the Liturgy of the Word, Christ speaking to us through the texts read there, now shifts to the altar for the Liturgy of the Eucharist.

That altar by its design and construction as well as by the items used upon it for worship symbolize that this is a place for both the holy sacrifice and the sacred banquet. It is both an altar for Christ's sacrifice and a table of the Lord. At one and the same time it recalls the Last Supper, re-presents the death of the Lord on Good Friday, and recreates Christ's Easter Sunday resurrection.

Catholic churches today locate altars near the people. Ordinarily they will be fixed and dedicated altars, freestanding so that the priest may walk around them and offer Mass facing the people. They should be situated in such a way that the attention of the whole congregation is drawn to and focuses upon the action at the altar.

The Church traditionally has insisted that the altar be of stone and preferably of natural stone. This links the altar representing Christ, the living stone, with biblical texts identifying Jesus in that fashion. The first letter of Peter, for example, urges that we "Come to him, a living stone . . ." (1 Peter 2:4). Paul's letter to the Ephesians teaches that the household of God is "built upon the foundation of the Apostles, with Christ himself as the capstone" (Ephesians 2:20).

Current Church directives, however, do permit moveable altars which can be transferred from place to place and made of other solid, becoming, and well-crafted materials. The use of stone and the establishment of a massive, permanently fixed altar does convey to those gathered for worship the security, reliability, and constancy of God, who is our rock and salvation, in whom we can place our total trust.

Relics of Saints

The Catholic Church has always shown great reverence for martyrs, those who have given their lives for the sake of Christ. An often-repeated adage in public worship maintains that the "blood of martyrs is the seed of Christians." Contemporary authors might cite in proof of this statement the case of the Korean martyrs, over one hundred Christians who were put to death between 1839 and 1867. Today the Korean church flourishes not only in that nation, but in other countries to which its citizens have emigrated. There are reportedly in the city of Toronto, Canada, alone, ten thousand Roman Catholic Koreans.

After Constantine's edict, there was an effort to build churches near or, if possible, directly over the graves of martyrs. We can see that in the example of St. Peter's at Rome, supposedly constructed over the remains of its patron saint.

In lieu of such a location, churches began to honor the martyrs by placing relics of those saints in the altar itself. This developed over the centuries into a custom and even a regulation that for a fixed or immovable altar there be a sepulcher, a small square or oblong cavity, in the top or side of the altar containing the relics of the saints. Current legislation urges maintaining this tradition of placing under the altar the dedicated relics of saints, even though the directive extends the possibility that the relics "even of non-martyrs" may be enclosed there. Our own cathedral, renovated about two decades ago, contains, to demonstrate this extension, the relics of St. Catherine Labouré and St. John Neumann, neither of whom was a martyr.

Necessary Altar Items

Many items are necessary for the sacrifice of the Mass at the altar and the distribution of Communion from this table of the Lord.

At least one *white cloth* should be placed upon the top or *mensa* of the altar. This could be a reminder of Christ's sacrifice on Calvary and the white cloths which surrounded his body as it was taken from the cross and buried in the tomb. It also reminds us that the Mass is at the same time a sacred banquet, a holy meal, a ritual surrounding Holy Communion for those assembled for the Mass.

The *corporal* is a square, white, folded linen cloth. It takes its name from the Latin word *corpus,* which means "body." The consecrated Body and Blood of Christ will soon rest upon this corporal, thus the name given to that unique cloth. The corporal usually has a cross woven into its center. It is ironed and folded in such a way that the cloth forms nine squares. In former days of intense religious symbolism, some viewed this as another image of the Trinity with the multiplication of threes and the one cloth. It should be large enough to accommodate all the vessels that will be brought to the altar.

The *purificator* is another white linen cloth often marked with a cross and carefully folded. As the name suggests, it is used to purify the sacred vessels, particularly the chalice.

The *chalice* will contain the wine mixed with water, ultimately to be transformed into the Precious Blood of Christ. Thus chalices should be made of worthy and durable materials. Traditionally these were fashioned of gold or silver with pertinent symbols or words engraved on their surfaces. In recent years, ceramic, wood, and even glass chalices have appeared—the last having the advantage of making the wine more visible.

A *dish, paten,* or *plate* holds the larger piece of unleavened bread, or host, for the priest presiding at the Mass as well as smaller particles for the congregation. There may also be additional larger containers of glass, metal, or other material when many people are expected.

Glass vessels for water and wine. Depending on the anticipated size of the congregation and the practice of the parish, there may be a large flagon of wine for the celebration. Before elevating the cup a little and blessing God for the gift of wine, the priest (or deacon) pours a few drops of water into the chalice or flagon of wine. As he does this, the priest (or deacon) says quietly,

> By the mystery of this water and wine may we come to share in the divinity of Christ, who humbled himself to share in our humanity.

Because of the distance from the altar and the quiet, almost silent recitation of those words, most members of the assembly may hardly notice and much less understand the significance of this highly symbolic action. It has a long and diverse history. An ancient rule, originating in Greece but practiced in Palestine during Christ's time, required that some water must be mingled even with the table wine. We find writings in the second century that mention this practice. That addition would naturally temper the wine. Over subsequent centuries the mingling by which the wine and water became inseparable took on a variety of symbolic meanings. This gesture thus came to symbolize among other truths:

- the union of divine and human elements in Christ;
- the descent of God's Son into this world becoming one of us;
- the close bond between Christ and his Church;
- the elevation of Christians, through baptism, to a sharing by grace of Jesus' divine nature;
- the pouring out of blood and water from the Savior's side on the cross;
- the intimate union of Christ and ourselves.

The mixing of water with wine is a minor action, but one that can symbolize many truths of the faith.

Pitcher, basin, and towel. Prior to and after the optional incensation, the priest performs two gestures and recites quietly phrases expressing humility, contrition, and the desire for a purified heart: (1) He bows from the waist and recites a brief prayer taken from one of the oldest formularies of the *Roman Missal;* based on Daniel 3:39, it begs God to receive and be pleased with the sacrifice that we offer "with humble and contrite hearts." (2) He moves to the side and washes his hands.

In early Christian centuries, the congregation brought not only bread, wine, and money, but food and other gifts for the church and the poor. The priest, after handling those gifts, understandably needed to cleanse his hands. That necessity no longer exists today, but the symbolic gesture, which has its roots in Jewish as well as early Christian traditions, continues to have value. We express our desire and need for inner purity as we begin this sacred and holy action. To achieve its full value, this symbolic gesture requires a deliberate action and the use of an easily visible pitcher, basin, and towel and an abundant supply of water. Both hands, not a few fingers, need washing in full view of the assembly.

During the 1570 Mass, the priest, inaudibly, recited an entire psalm as he washed his hands. The 1970 Mass simplifies this action by providing one verse only from Psalm 51: "Lord, wash away my iniquity; cleanse me from my sin."

Bells and smells. During the middle of the twentieth century some referred to Catholic churches as places of "bells and smells." They meant that servers frequently rang little bells during worship services and that the aroma of incense often filled the air. Those experiences are less common now as we move into the third millennium. Few parishes continue to have altar servers ring special bells at Mass. Incense is seldom used at Sunday Masses, being reserved for funerals and special devotional events.

There were no Church restrictions or prohibitions that caused this decline, only a combination of complex factors. Ironically, while bells and incense generally disappeared in Catholic liturgies, those two elements, especially the latter, grew in popularity in the secular American culture, particularly among young people.

The 1970 Mass directives still provide opportunities for the use of incense, with the preparation of gifts a major occasion for that action. There are two basic meanings to this gesture. First, those gently rising clouds of incense symbolize the Church's offering and our prayer rising to the sight of God. Both Old and New Testament biblical texts mention this practice and metaphor in worship services (Psalm 141:2; Revelation 8:4). Second, the gesture honors the object or persons being incensed. It recognizes the dignity (through creation and baptism) of each as well as the special presence of Christ in the priest celebrant, the ministers, and the rest of the assembly.

The 1570 Mass contained precise directions and accompanying words for the incensation of gifts and altar. Those have been omitted from the 1970 missal. We continue to incense altar and gifts as we did in the past, but simply with natural movements that reflect the symbolic meaning of the action.

Roman Catholics and visitors to our services most often experience the use of incense at funerals. Incensation is a more definitive part of the burial liturgy and includes incensing the cross, Easter candle, and casket. For this action to accomplish its purpose, there needs to be sufficient burning charcoal and incense to produce visible clouds emerging from the incensation vessel (called the thurible).

The *sacramentary* is moved from the chair to the altar for the Liturgy of the Eucharist.

We have already discussed the required presence of *candles*, symbolic of Christ, the light of the world, on or near the altar and the *cross* as well.

Catholic churches have a variety of *collection receptacles* for the gathering of offerings. In the early Christian centuries, the congregation brought forward real gifts more often than legal tender. Designated persons carried to the altar the bread, wine, and water as well as foodstuffs and other items for the poor. Over time these processions disappeared. The 1970 Mass restored the practice. It suggested that members of the congregation carry forward the bread and wine required as well as other gifts for the needs of the Church and the poor. The priest and deacon receiving these items place the eucharistic elements on the altar and the other gifts near, but not on, the altar. In a few American churches the entire congregation walks to the sanctuary and deposits individual gifts in receptacles near the altar.

Communion from the Cup

In most Roman Catholic churches today, there is no communion railing and the official posture for receiving Holy Communion is standing. Part of the reason for both the elimination of the rail and the standardization of standing is to facilitate receiving Communion from the cup or chalice. That process works much better for the minister of the cup and the recipient when each one stands.

Approaching the altar to receive Communion continues a fulfillment of the Lord's injunction to "take and eat," "take and drink." Thus, together we eat and drink the Body and Blood of Christ. The fuller sign of accomplishing this ideal involves drinking from the cup as well as eating the consecrated bread.

Luke's account of the Last Supper reminds us that "this cup is the new covenant in my blood, which will be shed for you" (Luke 22:20). Our drinking from the common cup means a deeper sharing in that covenant.

Matthew's account adds the prediction that, if we drink this cup with Jesus, we will one day share with Christ the heavenly banquet. "I tell you, from now on I shall not drink this fruit of the vine until the day when I drink it with you new in the kingdom of my Father" (Matthew 26:29).

Mark's account of James and John speaking with Jesus, seeking to sit in glory with Christ, one at his right and the other at his left, contains the Lord's subsequent warning and prediction: They will indeed have that reward, but only if they share in his cup of suffering and drink the chalice of pain with him. "The cup that I drink, you will drink . . ." (Mark 10:39). Drinking the Precious Blood from the cup gives us a fuller appreciation of being one with the suffering Christ, Jesus the abandoned one.

Offering the opportunity for everyone present to drink the Precious Blood from the cup is a currently encouraged ideal and a growing practice in parishes. However, the percentage of people taking advantage of that opportunity is relatively low, certainly less than a majority of worshipers.

A brief bit of history may be helpful here. The Christian Church from the outset until the thirteenth century in the West (continuing on to the present in the East) consistently and commonly distributed Communion under both kinds to the laity. Through those years and even today, this remains the fullest expression and most perfect fulfillment of what our Lord said, did, and directed. At the same time, the Church always gave Communion under one kind when circumstances so dictated and recognized this as a valid, complete, true sacrament. Thus the Eucharist was offered under the sign of bread alone to those confined at home, to the sick, to prisoners, or to monks living in isolation. Similarly Communion under the appearance of wine alone for infants and the gravely ill formed a standard and accepted custom throughout this period.

Practical difficulties and poor attitudes linked to produce a change in the thirteenth and fourteenth centuries. There was no denial (in fact there was greater affirmation) of the truth that each kind—bread or wine—contained the "whole" Christ, present body and blood, soul and divinity, in all the fullness and power of his life, sufferings, and resurrection. But the faithful, for complicated historical reasons, approached the sacraments much less frequently and, unfortunately, failed to realize fully that sacrifice and sacrificial meal are one in the Mass. These doctrinal and devotional attitudes, combined with contagion in times of rampant disease, the possibility of irreverence or spilling, the hesitation of some communicants to drink from a common cup, the large numbers at Easter and other special feasts, and the scarcity of wine in northern countries, led to a gradual abandonment of Communion under both species.

A reaction set in during the fourteenth century, and many

reformers urged a return to the early Christian tradition. However, in doing so some maintained that Communion under the sign of bread alone was invalid, a deprivation, an incomplete and erroneous compliance with the Lord's teaching in John's Gospel. Roman Catholics—both clergy and laity—bristled during those heated days in the face of these attacks and discouraged or forbade reintroduction of the practice under such controversial conditions.

The bishops at the Second Vatican Council urged return of Communion from the cup under appropriate circumstances. An instruction of June 29, 1970, from the Vatican Congregation for Divine Worship implemented that directive:

> In order that the fullness of sign in the eucharistic banquet may be seen more clearly by the faithful, the Second Vatican Ecumenical Council laid down that in certain cases—to be decided by the Holy See—the faithful should be able to receive holy communion under both kinds. This leaves intact the dogmatic principles recognized in the Council of Trent, by which it is taught that Christ whole and entire and the true sacrament are also received under one species alone.

More current regulations continue to encourage Communion from the cup and provide guidance for its proper administration. It is very desirable, as a fuller sign, that the communicant drink from the cup. But there is no obligation to do so, and the "whole" Christ is received under one sign alone, of bread or wine.

Visitors to Catholic churches at Mass time will probably notice off to the side additional empty cups, communion dishes, and purificators perhaps upon a tray for easy transport to the altar at communion time. Those who enter Roman Catholic churches outside of scheduled times for liturgical services will not see the necessary altar items. These are kept in a separate workroom or sacristy which may also double as a vesting area for the clergy. What they will observe in the sanctuary are three focal points: the presider's chair, the ambo or table of God's word from which the holy words are proclaimed, and the altar or table of God's body upon which the sacrifice of the Mass is offered and from which the Holy Eucharist is received.

Heroes and Heroines, Models and Helpers

The Italian Connection

Frances Xavier Cabrini possessed from earliest days an intense fear of water and drowning. Despite that great anxiety she still, for noble and religious reasons, crisscrossed the Atlantic over two dozen times during her lifetime from 1850 to 1917. Nor were the ships then as comfortable, fast, and safe as transoceanic vessels are today. She made those fear-filled journeys to find persons in her native Italy willing to come to the United States and serve, for the most part, Italian immigrants here in the United States.

Always frail in health, but deeply spiritual, Mother Cabrini, as she came to be known, dreamed in her childhood of becoming a missionary and laboring in China. Several years after she had worked in an orphanage as a religious sister, however, Church leaders sent her not east, but west to America for ministry with those who had migrated from Italy to the United States.

Not only was the initial voyage terrifying for Mother Cabrini, but she received a cold, almost hostile, reception from the archbishop of New York City. The residence for a proposed orphanage had not become available, and as a result the prelate suggested she go back to Italy. She respectfully listened to his recommendation, but with a determination fueled by her total dependence upon God moved ahead with her mission. Over the next thirty-five years, Mother Cabrini established sixty-seven institutions to care for the sick, the poor, the abandoned, the uneducated, and the immigrants who had come from Italy to find a new home. The saint died of malaria at a hospital she had founded in Chicago.

At her canonization in 1946, Pope Pius XII stated: "Although her constitution was very frail, her spirit was endowed with such singular strength that, knowing the will of God in her regard, she permitted nothing to impede her from accomplishing what seemed beyond the strength of a woman."

A metal bas-relief is attached to a wall in the vestibule area of St. Patrick's Cathedral in New York. It depicts Mother Cabrini with a trail of immigrants behind her, Italians recently arrived in the United States in need of help.

One of the tapestries at Our Lady of Angels Cathedral in Los Angeles contains an image of Mother Cabrini.

Frances Xavier Cabrini was the first United States citizen to be canonized. The Catholic Church celebrates her feast on November 13. This frail, but energetic, determined, and amazingly productive woman proves the effectiveness of total trust in God.

Chapter 6

Holy Oils

The Catholic Church cherishes its history and traditions. The consecration of oils for sacred purposes illustrates that reverence and maintenance of long-standing practices. By the third century, there already existed a custom of blessing three kinds of oil: Oil of Catechumens, Chrism, and Oil of the Sick.

This practice continues today. Every year, usually during Holy Week, the bishop of a diocese consecrates in his cathedral at a "Chrism Mass" three large containers of special oil, one for catechumens, one for chrism, and one for the sick. At the end of the liturgical celebration, delegates from every parish come forward and receive three small vessels containing a quantity of those different oils. Upon return to the parish, the delegates store receptacles in a dedicated compartment of the church where they can easily be retrieved throughout the coming year.

However, before the storage takes place, a priest or deacon of the parish pours a portion of each oil into smaller silver vessels for actual use with various sacraments in the months ahead. That includes a small metal container or "stock" packed with cotton over which is poured Oil of the Sick. Priests will carry this with them when they minister the sacrament of the anointing of the sick.

This extended procedure demonstrates the link between the people receiving the sacraments, the priest, the parish, the bishop, and through the bishop all the bishops of the world. The whole Church, as it were, is involved in every sacrament.

From left to right: Oil of the Sick, Oil of the Catechumens, and Sacred Chrism.

The oil for blessing has traditionally been olive oil. However, since in contemporary times it is often unobtainable or difficult to obtain in some parts of the world, the Church now permits another kind of oil, provided it is derived from plants and is thus similar to olive oil. Balsam or some type of perfume is added to the olive oil or its substitute to form the raw material for chrism.

Since the 1960s there has been a trend to focus attention in churches on the compartment or container for these holy oils. Prior to that, the location was a small cabinet in the church, sacristy, or vesting room hardly noticeable to people in the congregation.

The development in our own cathedral illustrates this shift. As we have mentioned earlier, the extensive renovation of the church interior included a separate, quite beautifully decorated baptistry with a wall compartment marked *Olea Sancta,* or "holy oils." Unfortunately, both items were constructed a decade too soon. Ten years later the revised *Rite of Baptism* called for a different location and type of font. The renewed interest and emphasis on the holy oils also emerged at that time.

A second major renovation in the late 1980s, this one designed to meet liturgical developments, provided a new baptismal font and a new container for the holy oils. The architect/designer located the holy oil container in the front of the church, at the side of the altar and next to the baptismal font. The two-to-three-foot-high glass receptacle rests on a granite pedestal with the stone matching similar material used for the font, presiding chair, ambo, and altar. The outline of the compartment mirrors the lines of the cathedral's exterior face. Constructed mostly of glass, it gives a clear view of the three large glass vessels containing the holy oils, each marked with the identifying initials: O.C., O.I., S.C. A spotlight focuses attention on the compartment, and lights built into the base of the compartment attractively illumine the three vessels.

During Holy Thursday night, the Blessed Sacrament is reserved on a side altar beyond the baptismal font and holy oils compartment. Several hundred people stop by the cathedral to make their prayerful "visit" to Christ reserved in this special way. As they approached that reposition shrine, the visitors must pass by both the font and the compartment, thus silently, yet visually, experiencing the connection between baptism, other sacraments, and the Eucharist.

Oil of the Catechumens

The vessel marked "O.C." (*Oleum Catechumenorum*) contains the Oil of the Catechumens. It is used for baptisms, mostly of infants, with the child anointed on the breast by the priest or deacon.

Just prior to the anointing, the priest or deacon recites this prayerful formula:

> We anoint you with the oil of salvation
> in the name of Christ our Savior;
> may he strengthen you
> with his power,
> who lives and reigns for ever and ever.

In ancient days, athletes in wrestling matches frequently anointed their entire bodies with oil to make them more elusive in the match with their opponent. Some would draw a parallel with this practice and consider one of the effects of baptism to be a strengthening of the person in the struggle against darkness and evil, a greater ability to elude the entrapments of Satan.

Sacred Chrism

The vessel marked "S.C." (*Sanctum Chrisma*) contains the Sacred Chrism. The blessed olive oil (or its substitute) contains balsam or some other perfume which gives it a certain fragrance. The Church uses holy chrism for three sacraments—baptism, confirmation, and ordination (which includes the ordaining of priests and bishops).

In baptism, the priest or deacon spreads the pleasant smelling oil on the top of the infant's head. Before the actual anointing he recites these words:

> God the Father of our Lord Jesus Christ has freed you from sin, given you a new birth by water and the Holy Spirit and welcomed you into his holy people. He now anoints you with the chrism of salvation. As Christ was anointed Priest, Prophet and King, so may you live always as a member of his body, sharing everlasting life.

The Jewish religious tradition anointed three persons: priests, prophets, and kings. Christ was the anointed of God, a priest, prophet, and king par excellence. Through baptism Christians possess the risen Jesus within them and thus share in his roles of priest, prophet, and king.

In the sacrament of confirmation, the bishop, or in certain circumstances a priest, anoints the candidate on the forehead pronouncing as he does so this brief formula: "Be sealed with the gift of the Holy Spirit." While the Holy Spirit enters the baptized person as part of the now indwelling Trinity, confirmation emphasizes the unique gifts of the Holy Spirit as they were poured out upon the apostles and believers assembled on Pentecost. They assure the recipient of the needed wisdom and strength to live the Christian life.

During the ordination liturgy, the consecrating or ordaining bishop anoints with chrism the palms of the man receiving priesthood and the head of the man receiving the episcopacy.

Oil of the Sick

The vessel marked "O.I." (*Oleum Infirmorum*) contains the Oil of the Sick. However, the use of this Oil of the Sick has varied in the Church's history.

The Church looks to the Bible as a foundation for this practice of anointing the sick with oil. It considers an incident in Mark's Gospel as an intimation of the sacrament. In that episode Jesus gathered the Twelve and sent them out two by two to preach the good news. At the conclusion of this section, "the mission of the Twelve," Mark tells us: "So they went off and preached repentance. They drove out many demons, and they anointed with oil many who were sick and cured them" (Mark 6:6-13).

The Church sees in the letter of James a recommendation and revelation of this practice and sacrament. Under a section entitled "Anointing of the Sick," we read:

> Is anyone among you suffering? He should pray. Is anyone in good spirits? He should sing praise. Is anyone among you sick? He should summon the presbyters of the church, and

they should pray over him and anoint him with oil in the name of the Lord, and the prayer of faith will save the sick person, and the Lord will raise him up. If he has committed any sins, he will be forgiven. (James 5:13-15)

In its introductory instruction to the *Rite for the Anointing of the Sick,* the Church understandably refers to the biblical foundations for this sacrament.

The priest addresses the ill person and others present in these words when ministering the sacrament outside of Mass:

My dear friends, we are gathered here in the name of our Lord Jesus Christ who is present among us. As the gospels relate, the sick came to him for healing; moreover he loves us so much that he died for our sake.

After citing the command of James quoted above, the instruction concludes: "Let us therefore commend our sick brother/sister to the grace and power of Christ, that he may save him and raise him/her up."

When the priest ministers to a sick individual the three sacraments of penance, anointing, and Eucharist in continuous fashion, he may employ this alternative instruction:

Beloved in Christ, the Lord Jesus is with us at all times, warming our hearts with his sacramental grace. Through his priests he forgives the sins of the repentant; he strengthens the sick through holy anointing; to all who watch for his coming, he gives the food of his body and blood to sustain them on their last journey, confirming their eternal life. Our brother/sister has asked to receive these three sacraments; let us help him/her with our love and our prayers.

In the first Christian centuries, the Church stressed that this sacrament was administered primarily to restore sick persons to health, enabling them once again to rejoin the community for the celebrations of Mass or the Eucharist.

During the Middle Ages, the focus shifted, with the emphasis now upon the sacrament as a preparation for death and eternity. It became known popularly as the "last rites" and its more formal title, "extreme unction," conveyed the notion that this was the last or final anointing before departure from the present world.

In the last half of the twentieth century, the Church partially returned to the teaching and practice of those early centuries. Still intended only for seriously ill persons, the anointing of the sick retained the notion of preparation for death, but now also restored the concept of return to health. The recipient no longer needs to be in "danger of death" or "perilously ill." Instead the word in the revised ritual is "serious"; this means that a person whose health is seriously impaired by sickness or old age could and should receive the sacrament. Someone with a head cold would not be eligible for the anointing; someone facing major surgery would. Someone with a simple stomach ache would not be eligible; an elderly individual in a nursing home or health-care facility could receive the sacrament.

The sacrament of the anointing of the sick, according to the 1983 ritual, gives the grace of the Holy Spirit to its recipients. That grace helps the ill individual to bear suffering bravely, to resist temptation of the Evil One, and to let go of anxieties about death. It also restores physical health, if that would be beneficial to the sick person's salvation and may bring forgiveness of sins to the one who is ill.

The ritual fundamentally involves the laying on of hands by the priest, the offering of a prayer of faith, and the anointing with Oil of the Sick.

The priest ordinarily anoints the forehead and the palms of the recipient's hands, reciting as he does so this essential formula:

(forehead)
Through this holy anointing may the Lord in his love and mercy help you with the grace of the Holy Spirit.

(hands)
May the Lord who frees you from sin save you and raise you
up.

Prayers after the anointing, recited when several are being
anointed simultaneously, plead for the positive effects of the
sacrament.

Father in heaven,
through this holy anointing
grant our brothers and sisters comfort in their suffering.
When they are afraid, give them courage,
when afflicted, give them patience,
when dejected, offer them hope,
and when alone, assure them of the support
of your holy people.

Lord Jesus Christ, our Redeemer,
by the grace of your Holy Spirit
cure the weakness of your servants.
Heal their weakness and forgive their sins;

expel all afflictions of mind and body;
mercifully restore them to full health,
and enable them to resume their former duties,
for you are Lord for ever and ever.

A Catholic church, both the building itself and everything
within it, points to something more, something beyond us, something quite transcendent. The sacraments as powerful symbols
also uniquely connect us with a divine presence. The risen Christ
is truly present, concealed, yet revealed, under various elements:
holy water, the spoken word, blessed bread and wine, the laying on
of hands, and consecrated oil. Through them we can reach the
awesome, distant God who is, at the same time, caring and close
to us.

Heroes and Heroines, Models and Helpers

The African and American Connection

Two saints of the Roman Catholic Church, one in Africa and one in Peru, serve as an inspiration for us to work on behalf of religious unity and racial harmony.

In the late 1900s King Mwanga of Uganda invited back to his country some Christian missionaries. But soon afterward his attitude changed; and, after accusing a group of Christians together with their Anglican bishop of espionage, he ordered them murdered. Later the king had a court page and a few other attendants beheaded because they "prayed from a book." Next he turned his attention to Charles Lwanga and twenty-one others, making immoral demands of them. With Charles as their leader, they all refused. The king, infuriated by this rejection, had Charles tortured terribly and on June 3, 1886, burned to death. He commanded the other twenty-one also to be killed and, subsequently, put to death a hundred Catholics and Protestants.

Pope Paul VI canonized these twenty-two Ugandan martyrs at the Second Vatican Council in 1964 and set June 3 as their feast day. He also declared St. Charles Lwanga as patron of black African youth.

The father of St. Martin de Porres (1579-1639) was a Spanish grandee, or nobleman of the highest rank, who later became governor of Panama. His union, outside of marriage, with a freed woman of Panama, probably black but also possibly of Native American stock, brought forth Martin and later a sister. Because Martin inherited the features and dark complexion of his mother, the father resented that development, never acknowledged his son until he was eight years old, and ultimately abandoned the family after the birth of Martin's sister.

Martin became a pharmacist, a nurse, a Dominican lay

brother, and ultimately, a Dominican religious. Deeply spiritual and a recognized mystic, he also was passionately dedicated to the service of the poor, so much so that they called him "Martin the charitable."

When Pope John XXIII canonized him in 1962, establishing November 3 as his feast day, he said of St. Martin: "He tried with all his might to redeem the guilty; lovingly he comforted the sick; he provided food, clothing and medicine for the poor; he helped as best he could, farm laborers and Negroes, as well as mulattos, who were looked upon at that time as akin to slaves. . . ."

Part III

From the Heart

Chapter 7

Sin and Forgiveness

Personal sin happens when we fail to follow the divine imperative within our hearts. In simpler terms, God says inside of us, "Do this," and we don't do it; or God says inside of us, "Don't do this," and we do it. That sinful disobedience can be of a major or a minor dimension. We lose our temper a bit, make a critical remark about another, or steal a small amount from a wealthy person. These are wrong actions but still of lesser moment or harm. We commit adultery, murder another, or steal a significant sum from a poor person. These wrong actions are of major moment and seriously injure others.

The major sins, usually called mortal sins, break our relationship with God; the minor sins, generally called venial sins, mar and weaken our relationship with God, but do not rupture the bond between us.

Guilt follows sin. Guilt is a painful and penetrating reality. One contemporary psychologist maintains that unacknowledged and unexpiated guilt is the ultimate source of all inner anguish. Guilt can keep us awake at night, cause an upset stomach, deprive us of peace. It clouds a beautiful day and stifles joy. Guilt may lead to an excessive preoccupation with ourselves and a forgetfulness of others. This pervasive and perduring pain, however, can also make us yearn intensely for forgiveness of sin and the lifting of guilt.

The Catholic Church in its teaching and practices balances two connected inner attitudes: it blends the honest recognition that we do sin and are sinners with total confidence that God, who came to save sinners, not to condemn them, is always ready to forgive our sins and free us from our guilt.

This teaching and practice has a sound biblical basis. The Hebrew Scriptures often describe God as slow to anger, kind and merciful, very careful not to break the bruised reed or snuff out the smoldering wick. The angel names the child born at Christmas Jesus, which means savior, "because he will save his people from their sins" (Matthew 1:21). During his public ministry Jesus often preached about forgiveness and forgave. In the Gospel of Luke, Christ speaks about the lost sheep, the lost coin, and the lost son with the comforting concluding words, "there will be more joy in heaven over one sinner who repents than over ninety-nine righteous people who have no need of repentance" (Luke 15:7). Jesus forgave the criminal on the cross, the woman caught in adultery, the woman known as a sinner, and the paralyzed young man.

The cross or crucifix, of course, dramatizes Christ's supreme act of love, his dying on Calvary for love of us, for the forgiveness of our sins. As we have described earlier, a large crucifix stands in the sanctuary near the altar in clear view of the people. That familiar symbol brings the action which took place on Good Friday to the attention of those in church and can inspire their prayerful meditation. Roman Catholics, however, also have another popular devotion which focuses on the suffering, death, and resurrection of Jesus Christ.

Stations of the Cross

In most, if not all, Catholic churches, a series of symbols on the walls of the nave represent the journey of Christ on Good Friday along the *via dolorosa,* or sorrowful way, to his crucifixion at Calvary. Those fourteen representations may be simple crosses with the number of each station upon them or actual artistic recreations of each particular scene.

Fourteen or fifteen stations of the cross recreate Jesus' sorrowful journey or *via dolorosa* from condemnation to crucifixion to resurrection.

Making the stations of the cross is not a required prayer nor a liturgical service, but a devotion for those who wish to use it. The journey can be made privately on an individual basis or publicly with a group of people led by a priest, deacon, or spiritual leader in the parish. While not as popular today as it was in the first part of the last century, the way of the cross still attracts people, particularly during the Lenten season. Parishes usually offer a public celebration of the stations with common prayers and song once a week during Lent, often on a Friday in remembrance of the crucifixion. Individuals frequently can also be seen throughout the day moving quietly from station to station, pausing at each one for prayer and reflection.

The traditional stations begin with Pilate's condemnation of Christ and conclude with Jesus being laid in the tomb. During the second half of the last century, many added a fifteenth station, the resurrection of Jesus, to this journey, although frequently there was no artistic representation of this scene as part of the series.

Here are the traditional fourteen stations of the cross plus the fifteenth one:

First station: Jesus is condemned to death
Second station: Jesus carries his cross
Third station: Jesus falls the first time
Fourth station: Jesus meets his afflicted mother
Fifth station: Simon of Cyrene helps Jesus to carry his cross
Sixth station: Veronica wipes the face of Jesus
Seventh station: Jesus falls the second time
Eighth station: Jesus meets the women of Jerusalem
Ninth station: Jesus falls a third time
Tenth station: Jesus is stripped of his clothes
Eleventh station: Jesus is nailed to the cross
Twelfth station: Jesus dies on the cross
Thirteenth station: the body of Jesus is taken down from the cross
Fourteenth station: Jesus is laid in the tomb
Fifteenth station: the resurrection of Jesus

On Good Friday, 1991, Pope John Paul II, according to long-standing papal tradition, led a crowd of people at the Roman Colosseum through the stations of the cross. He changed the format, however, altering the fourteen stations and adding a fifteenth. Some of the traditional ones were kept, while others were dropped and new ones inserted. All of the stations the Holy Father used had as their basis incidents recorded in the Gospels.

Here are these "Stations of the Cross with Pope John Paul II," including the biblical reference for each station:

First station: the agony of Jesus in the Garden of Olives (Mark 14:32-36)

Second station: the betrayal and arrest of Jesus (Mark 14:43-46)

Third station: the Sanhedrin condemns Jesus (Mark 14:55, 60-63)

Fourth station: Peter denies Jesus (Mark 14:66-72)

Fifth station: Pilate condemns Jesus to the cross (Mark 15:1, 6-15)

Sixth station: Jesus is scourged and crowned with thorns (John 19:1-3)

Seventh station: Jesus is mocked by the soldiers and given his cross (Mark 15:16, 18a, 19-20)

Eighth station: Simon the Cyrenian helps Jesus carry his cross (Mark 15:21)

Ninth station: Jesus meets the women of Jerusalem (Luke 23:27-28)

Tenth station: Jesus is crucified (Mark 15:22-24)

Eleventh station: Jesus promises paradise to the penitent criminal (Luke 23:33, 39-43)

Twelfth station: Jesus speaks to his mother and to his disciple (John 19:25-27)

Thirteenth station: Jesus dies on the cross (Mark 15:33-37)

Fourteenth station: the burial of Jesus (Mark 15:42-46)

Fifteenth station: Jesus rises from the dead (Mark 16:1-6)

Since these stations according to Pope John Paul II are of relatively recent origin, few churches have representations of them on their interior walls, although some are beginning to create such images. Many retreat centers have outdoor stations of the cross, but those would be rare in parishes.

The crucifix and stations of the cross point to something beyond what is represented on these objects. They fundamentally lead people to ponder the enormous love of Jesus Christ for them, a love manifested by his suffering and death endured that all might be forgiven their sins and freed from their guilt.

Chapels of Reconciliation

Up until the 1960s, in every Catholic church there was a confessional or several confessionals. Those confessionals, sometimes termed confession "boxes," typically had a center cubicle for the priest with openings at ear level on either side. A curtain or door concealed the priest, although his name was usually indicated over the entrance to the cubicle. The interior normally would be darkened, but the priest-confessor could turn on a light for reading when he was not occupied with penitents.

The penitents, or persons making their confessions, would kneel in a cubicle on either side of the priest, an area also darkened, with a door or heavy curtain at its entrance. The square opening at face level generally had a screen or lattice providing better anonymity for the penitent. These was also a small moveable wooden partition covering the aperture on either side. The priest closed one and opened the other to hear that person's confession; then reversed the process for the penitent on the other side. Since there were frequently great numbers and long lines, those double confessionals with a sliding partition speeded up the procedure. While one was confessing, the person on the opposite side, having finished, left and the next penitent entered the cubicle.

A significant shift occurred in 1973 with the publication of the revised *Rite of Penance*. Its recommendation for a biblical reading and the possible extension of hands during the confession ritual prompted the development of confession rooms or, better, chapels of reconciliation. These spaces provided penitents with the option of the anonymity behind the customary screen procedure or the new face-to-face across from the priest arrangement for the sacrament. Later the American bishops approved these chapels of reconciliation for use in the United States, a decision subsequently approved by Church authorities in Rome.

The following description illustrates one parish's efforts in the 1970s to convert a seldom used, windowless room into an attrac-

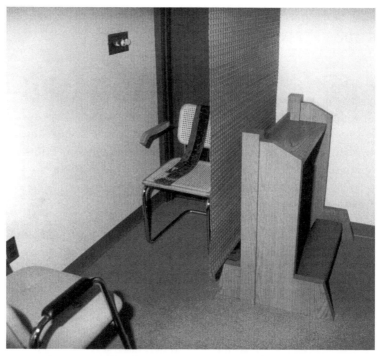

Reconciliation chapels offer in a comfortable and confidential space the option of kneeling anonymously or sitting across from the confessor in a face-to-face setting.

tive chapel of reconciliation. This type of renovation has been replicated in many parishes throughout the United States.

> We were trying to create a more suitable environment for the sacrament of Penance. So often the traditional "boxes" are dark and cramped, making some feel closed in and others frightened. The box-type confessionals presume an unnatural whispering and normally preclude any visual contact between priest and penitent. Those who have trouble kneeling or wish to speak at length with the confessor must endure an awkward, uncomfortable, perhaps painful ordeal. Making confession a happy, peaceful meeting in faith

with the merciful Jesus frequently becomes impossible simply because of the physical layout and atmosphere in which
this dialogue takes place.

Environmentally, then, we wanted our room to express a
simplicity of comfort, joy, quietness and dignity. But we also
sought to provide three alternatives for persons seeking
peace through penance; to confess anonymously, kneeling
behind a grill; to confess behind this screen, but seated in a
comfortable chair; to confess face-to-face in a conference
area further into the room beyond the partition.

To break the windowless character of the space, two walls
were painted in different, blending colors and the other two
in off-white and matte. Wall-to-wall carpeting was laid to
add warmth to the room.

A massive 5' x 7' wooden screen or grate was constructed
and bolted to the floor and one wall.

The screen serves a double function. First, it offers penitents
the customary kneeling spot for confessions of that kind, yet
with the advantage of actually seeing the priest through
these inch-square apertures. In this arrangement a person
no longer confesses to a blank wall or an opaque screen but
to a confessor whose features are easily discernible. The penitent remains, however, unseen and is given further visual
assurance of anonymity since the priest sits facing away
from the grill.

Those unable to kneel with ease (e.g., pregnant women, persons advanced in age, individuals with lengthy confessions)
may sit, still in the protected secrecy of that area, in a chair
located next to the screen.

The screen also acts as a divider marking off two-thirds of
the space as a conference section for face-to-face reconcilia-

tion. Upon entering the confessional room an individual feels an invitation to walk past the screen into this more brightly illumined, beautifully appointed portion.

The designers gave serious thought and great care to the question of lighting. The room used to be evenly lit by fluorescents, shadowless and uncomplimentary to the warmth of skin colors. Two incandescent floor lamps now provide a warm light there and simultaneously cast a subdued shadow over the screened confession area.

A rich 6' x 9' oriental rug in this section creates a sense of unity and visually invites one into the space.

A handsome 3' x 3' table, imported from Switzerland, gives the conference area a sense of place, a form to gather around. Two chairs and a small upright crucifix on the table complete the furnishings.

Those well versed in the art of counseling might object to the use of a table intervening between priest and penitent or question the straight, firm chairs and prefer soft, easy ones. To the contrary, our lengthy experience justifies the artist's recommendations.

Going to confession, even in face-to-face, conversational fashion, is not the same as seeking assistance from a guidance counselor or clinical psychologist. It's much easier to play games in the latter cases, although to do so would be an expensive and ultimately unproductive bit of recreation. Persons who seek the sacrament of penance do so presumably because they wish to reach God through his instrument, the priest. They know dishonesty with the confessor is tantamount to flouting the Lord. In my 18 years as a priest I have witnessed few, perhaps no instances where a penitent seemed artificial or deceptive. People like that normally avoid the confessional experience.

My point here is this: a sinner searching for forgiveness and peace makes himself vulnerable, opens up, exposes a basically unpleasant part of himself. The person thinks: "I am not terribly happy with myself for doing this, thinking that, neglecting something else." Admitting fault and guilt to another human is hard enough, even brutal; to do so face-to-face requires added courage and means a further unveiling of the real me.

An encounter in the conference area of our confessional room must, consequently, create in some a sense of inner spiritual nakedness. The table eases that frightening feeling. It provides a place for the hands, something to hang on to, an object to hide behind.

The tiny table cross has become an unexpectedly potent part of the room. Our eyes speak volumes. The nervous penitent can't always look directly at the priest, especially in the early moments of a confession. So he or she glances here, there, everywhere: at the confessor, over his head, around the warm but plainly painted and decorated room; then, finally, the vision fixes on a body nailed to the cross. The crucifix says it all. "Father, forgive them. . . . Greater love than this. . . . I came to save sinners, not the just. . . . Your sins are forgiven, go in peace. . . ."

Important to any architectural space, or room, is its entrance. We gave careful consideration to what symbol should be employed as an indication of the priest's presence. A thick (2½") candle seemed best. It symbolizes Christ present in this sacrament of peace and recalls the paschal candle with its complex, multiple liturgical usage—for Holy Saturday and Easter time, for baptisms and funerals, for death (to sin) and resurrection (to life).

When a person confesses anonymously behind the partition or screen, the priest simply extends his right hand in the direction of the penitent; when confessing face-to-face, the priest may offer the option of simply raising his right hand or of extending his hands over the head of the penitent. In either scenario the priest then pronounces these words of forgiveness:

> God, the Father of mercies, through the death and resurrection of his Son has reconciled the world to himself and sent the Holy Spirit among us for the forgiveness of sins; through the ministry of the Church, may God give you pardon and peace, and I absolve you from your sins in the name of the Father, and of the Son, and of the Holy Spirit.

Pardon and peace, the forgiveness of sins, and the lifting of guilt. A crucifix, the stations of the cross, and chapels of reconciliation connect Catholics with the gentle, kind, and merciful God who bestows pardon and peace upon repentant sinners, forgives their transgressions, and heals their feelings of guilt.

Heroes and Heroines, Models and Helpers

The Polish Connection

Maximilian Mary Kolbe (1894-1941) was born in Poland and as a very devout young boy believed that Mary, the mother of Jesus, appeared to him. In the apparition, Mary held in her hands two crowns, one white, one red, one for purity and one for martyrdom. The angelic woman asked if he would like to have one of them. Maximilian responded, "I choose both." The woman smiled and disappeared.

At the age of sixteen he entered the Franciscan community, obtained graduate degrees in philosophy and theology, possessed a great interest in science, and was finally ordained a priest. Because of his devotion to the mother of Jesus, he inserted "Mary" in his name.

He preached and taught in Poland, then in Japan, but he returned to his native land as the Nazi armies overran that country.

In 1941 Nazi leaders arrested Kolbe and sent him to the concentration camp at Auschwitz. Soon after his arrival, a prisoner escaped from the camp. In a typical reprisal, the commandant decreed that ten men would die. As the prisoners were lined up and the soldier moved along randomly selecting those who would perish, Maximilian Kolbe, Number 16670, stepped forward.

He said to the commandant, "I would like to take that man's place. He has a wife and children."

The surprised soldier asked: "Who are you?"

Kolbe simply answered: "A priest."

The commandant accepted the exchange and sent the ten condemned men to a cellar prison, had them stripped naked, and left the victims to die of starvation.

Maximilian Kolbe inspired his companions to pray and sing hymns instead of screaming in terror. When four remained alive, the jailer took a hypodermic needle and injected carbonic acid into the priest's arm, causing instant death. His body and those of the nine others were then taken to the crematory ovens for burning.

The Church declared St. Maximilian Mary Kolbe a saint in 1982 and established the date of his death, August 14, the eve of the Assumption of Mary, for his feast.

Pope John Paul II believes that the human heart will only be content when it is self-giving. St. Maximilian models that total giving of self for others.

Chapter 8

A Special Presence

The currents of air in a room will cause a prism suspended from the ceiling to twist and turn. When rays of sunlight strike the moving prism, it reflects a variety of colors and sends off the reflections in different directions. There is a parallel between that phenomenon and our examination of certain mysteries in the Roman Catholic tradition. We need to turn the mysteries around and view them from various vantage points if we are to gain a fuller appreciation of their riches.

The Eucharist is a case in point. We can consider this great gift from God as a sacrifice, a sacrament, and a presence. It is at one and the same time the sacrifice of the Mass, the sacrament or sacred meal of Christ's Body and Blood to be received in Holy Communion, and the special presence of the risen Lord reserved in a tabernacle for our prayer of adoration. Concentrating on one dimension of the Eucharist and ignoring the others gives us an incomplete and sometimes even a distorted notion of this mystery. Considering all three aspects of the Eucharist gives us a fuller and balanced grasp of that wonderful gift from God.

Tabernacle

In the early Christian centuries, some bread consecrated at Mass was set aside and reserved in a worthy place for later distribution to the sick confined at home or to prisoners restricted to their quarters. Around the Middle Ages, devotion to the special or Real

Presence of Christ in those consecrated hosts began to develop. This resulted in more elaborate containers for the reserved hosts called tabernacles, chapels for eucharistic adoration and ceremonies honoring the risen Lord present in a larger consecrated host.

This slightly larger circular host would on occasion be removed from the tabernacle and placed in the center of an upright decorated receptacle called the monstrance or ostensarium (from Latin words meaning "to show" or "to display"). Catholics would then express their devotion to the Lord "exposed" before them in the monstrance, which was surrounded by a cluster of lighted candles. This exposition of the Blessed Sacrament would extend frequently for an hour (a "holy hour"), once a year for forty hours (the "Forty-Hours Devotion"), and on occasion be carried in procession within or outside the church preceded by servers swinging thuribles of burning incense.

In subsequent centuries tabernacles were located on the main altar or in a central position of the sanctuary. To alert those visiting the church that the Blessed Sacrament was reserved in the tabernacle, a substantial sanctuary candle (or candles), often in a red casing, situated near the tabernacle, burned day and night. Catholics entering the church and observing the lighted sanctuary lamp would genuflect on one knee in the aisle toward the tabernacle before taking their place in the pews or chairs. By doing so, they were expressing with their bodies their faith in Christ's presence.

This arrangement of the tabernacle in the center of the sanctuary with burning lamp nearby and the practice of genuflecting before the tabernacle upon entering a Catholic church was a standard feature and procedure in the United States during the first half of the twentieth century.

A Shift in Focus

During the second half of the last century, prompted by the liturgical renewal and the directives of the Second Vatican Council, there was a shift in eucharistic focus. Without denying the Real Presence or the value of devotion to Jesus present in the tabernacle, official Church teaching emphasized as well the presence of Christ in the action of the Mass. As we have seen, the bishops gathered in Rome proclaimed the multiple presences of Christ not only in the Eucharist as Real Presence, but also in the Eucharist as sacrifice and sacrament, in the proclamation of the Scriptures, in the celebration of the sacraments, and where two or three gather in the Lord's name.

That shift produced significant changes in the arrangement of the sanctuary. The tabernacle generally was transferred to another location, often to a side altar, near enough for easy access during Mass when needed and also readily accessible for personal, private devotion.

The focal points in the sanctuary, as noted earlier, now became the presiding chair, the ambo, and the altar. Moreover, designers generally made an attempt to bring the people closer to and more intimately linked with the sanctuary since Christ was also uniquely present in the midst of those gathered in his name. Since standing to receive the Eucharist was now the officially endorsed posture, that frequently meant removal of the communion railing in older churches.

Church Directives

The July 2000 revised *Roman Missal* provides direction for the nature and location of the tabernacle. As a rule there will be only one tabernacle in the church, and it should be immovable and made of solid, unbreakable, and opaque material. The tabernacle must also be kept locked to avoid the danger of desecration. It should be located in a part of the church that is noble, worthy, conspicuous, well decorated, and suitable for prayer.

A designated lamp, burning continuously near the tabernacle and fed with oil or wax, indicates and honors the presence of Christ within the tabernacle.

An immovable tabernacle of solid, unbreakable, and opaque material, placed on a pedestal or altar within the main church or in a special chapel of reservation, contains consecrated hosts for distribution to the sick or, if necessary, for use at Mass. The tabernacle is also a location for private adoration of the Real Presence in the Eucharist.

The tabernacle should *not* be on the altar on which Mass is celebrated. It could be placed in the sanctuary, but apart from the altar of sacrifice. It may also be located in another chapel, integrally connected with the church and conspicuous to the people, suitable for adoration and the private prayer of the faithful (Articles 314-316).

The sanctuaries and tabernacles of newly constructed and renovated older churches usually reflect the shift we have described and conform to these official Church directives.

Earlier in this book we described the new church in the suburbs of Fargo, North Dakota. That structure includes such a chapel for the Blessed Sacrament, but one designed with direct outside access to make feasible around-the-clock adoration of the reserved eucharistic Christ.

Bread of Angels

At occasional celebrations in a Catholic church—weddings, funerals, certain solemn occasions—a soloist or choir may sing the famous Latin piece *Panis Angelicus*. That hymn of praise centers around this "angelic bread," or bread of angels, the Holy Eucharist.

The song enjoys a rich biblical basis. In the Hebrew Scriptures, the Jewish people complained in the desert to Moses about their hunger and lack of food. He brought this complaint to God, who responded with the miraculous manna from heaven. In the Christian Scriptures, the sixth chapter of John's Gospel, Jesus connects his promise of the Eucharist to that unique manna. He is and will be the bread of life, the true bread come down from heaven, the bread which assures life everlasting to those who eat it.

We associate angels with things heavenly and thus the connection between the Eucharist and angelic beings.

Our century-old cathedral in Syracuse, mirroring the type of interiors in older churches, contains many images of angels. The large rose window over the front entrance contains eight circles with an angel in each surrounding the major circular portion. The central stained glass window in the apse represents Mary and her Immaculate Conception, the patron and title of the cathedral, with a cluster of angels at her feet. Murals along each side portray angels holding symbols of a particular title honoring Mary, the mother of Jesus. Other windows contain cherubic figures in them.

References to angels and representations of them in the interiors of new Catholic churches seemed to disappear in the middle of the last century. Some apparently judged angels to be a medieval, outdated, almost embarrassing part of Catholicism's tradition. That elimination or omission curiously occurred about the same time that our American culture rediscovered angels. Books about them, television shows featuring angels, and angelic jewelry became the rage in the United States. *Time* magazine, reflecting that trend, dedicated a cover story to the subject of angels.

While popular devotions and church decorations no longer featured angels as much, Church teaching and practices continued to uphold both their existence and importance in Catholic tradition.

A side wall mural invokes Mary's prayerful assistance with an angel underneath holding a plaque containing the symbol of that invocation—a rosary.

The *Catechism of the Catholic Church,* issued under the signature of Pope John Paul II in 1992, contains an eight-paragraph section entitled "The Angels." It states in the first line that the existence of spiritual non-corporeal beings, usually called angels in Sacred Scripture, is a truth of faith. The concluding paragraph mentions that angels surround human life from its beginning until death with their watchful care and protection. It also teaches that an angel stands beside each believer as a protection and shepherd leading the person to life (Articles 328-336).

Popular prayers and official worship continue to mention these angelic creatures. Older Catholics will remember the Guardian Angel prayer, "Angel of God my guardian dear . . . ," memorized as a youth, but probably no longer recited regularly, if at all. The Church calendar celebrates the feast of Guardian Angels and with more solemnity honors the archangels, Gabriel, Michael, and Raphael. Every Mass includes the angelic hymn, "Holy, holy, holy. . . ." Funerals conclude with, "May the angels take you into paradise."

It will be interesting to see if Catholic church interiors in the future resurrect this once strong, currently dormant, yet culturally popular devotion to angels.

The book of Psalms reminds us that God is near to the brokenhearted and close to those who are crushed in spirit. The special presence of Christ in the Eucharist, but also the protective presence of angels around us, makes that nearness and closeness a reality. It takes, however, a faith which looks beyond to experience these presences in our lives.

Heroes and Heroines, Models and Helpers

The Asian Connection

For centuries the Catholic Church has repeated this axiom: "The blood of martyrs is the seed of Christians." That truth has been exemplified in both Korea and Japan where victims of martyrdom have given birth to thousands accepting the Christian message.

In 1984, Pope John Paul II visited Korea and there declared over one hundred persons to be saints who had suffered violent deaths as martyrs in that land between 1839 and 1867. Some were bishops and priests, but most were lay persons, forty-seven women and forty-five men.

The Christian faith was established there and grew in its early years through the efforts primarily of lay persons because no priests were able to enter the country.

The Church expanded rapidly after these martyrdoms. Today, to illustrate, there are four million Catholics in Korea and ten thousand Korean Catholics in Toronto, Canada, alone.

Pope John Paul II spoke about this remarkable faith phenomenon at the canonization of Andrew Kim Taegon, Paul Chong Hasong, and their companions.

> The Korean Church is unique because it was founded entirely by lay people. This fledgling Church, so young and yet so strong in faith, withstood wave after wave of fierce persecution. Thus, in less than a century, it could boast of 10,000 martyrs. The death of these martyrs became the leaven of the Church and led to today's splendid flowering of the Church in Korea. Even today their undying spirit sustains the Christians in the Church of silence in the north of this tragically divided land.

Pope John Paul II established September 20 as their feast day.

Nagasaki, Japan, is familiar to Americans as the city upon which the United States dropped the second atomic bomb. However, near that same city 350 years earlier, in 1597, a group of twenty-six Christians were crucified, attached to crosses by ropes and chains, with their deaths achieved by the thrust of a lance. The victims were clergy, catechists, and lay people. Brother Paul Miki, a Jesuit and native of Japan, is the best known. St. Paul Miki preached this final sermon suspended upon the cross and scheduled for execution.

The sentence of judgment says these men came to Japan from the Philippines, but I did not come from any other country. I am a true Japanese. The only reason for my being killed is that I have taught the doctrine of Christ. I certainly did teach the doctrine of Christ. I thank God it is for this reason I die. I believe that I am telling only the truth before I die. I know you believe me and I want to say to you all once again: Ask Christ to help you to become happy. I obey Christ. After Christ's example I forgive my persecutors. I do not hate them. I ask God to have pity on all, and I hope my blood will fall on my fellow men as a fruitful rain.

When missionaries finally returned to Japan about two centuries later, they discovered thousands of Christians around Nagasaki who had secretly preserved the faith. St. Paul Miki's blood indeed did fall as a fruitful rain upon the people of Japan.

The Church celebrates the feast of St. Paul Miki and his companions on February 6 and holds up these two groups of Asian martyrs from Korea and Japan as models of faith for us today.

The tapestries in the Cathedral of Our Lady of Angels in Los Angeles contain sketches of both St. Andrew Kim Taegon and St. Paul Miki.

Chapter 9

From the Visible
to the Invisible

A colleague at work and a married couple who have been very close friends for years recently became grandparents for the first time. They carry with them at all times and are anxious to display with joyful pride photos of the newly arrived grandchildren.

On the top of a file cabinet in my office stands a framed photo of two high school students, dressed formally, at their senior prom. They had their own dates, but got together and posed in this picture as a gift for me. Both had worked for several years on a part-time basis at our church and in the fall would be off to college. This note accompanied that photo:

> Thank you for being one of the most important people in our lives since the day we were born. You have helped us to see the ways in which God works in our world and have shown us how important it is to believe. We have both enjoyed working at the Cathedral and can honestly say that we've probably received more back than we've given to our faith community. The Cathedral has also brought us together as really close friends . . . we've already got it planned out—U of R and RIT are exactly 8 minutes away from entrance to entrance . . . we're going to meet every Sunday and go to church together to keep our faith and

friendship alive. Thank you for being such a key part of our lives. We'll miss you as we go to college but will never lose touch. Love always.

The editors of a book I wrote fifteen years ago wanted this beautifully illustrated text to have, in addition, an artist's sketch to accompany the beginning of each chapter. Chapter 3, "Our Roots," contained an introductory story about my parents. A sketch of my father and mother, made from fifty-year-old photographs greets the reader. When I first viewed the sketches, I choked up a bit, much to my surprise, obviously touched by the memories these illustrations evoked within me.

Neither the grandparents nor I worship these photos or adore them. They are merely reminders of the real persons captured here in film or print. Those visible photos or sketches call to mind people who are not currently present in our midst and thus actually invisible to us. They help keep these individuals alive in our consciousness.

A parallel exists in the traditions of the Catholic Church. The Church frequently employs visible items—statues, images, symbols—to lead us to the invisible realities behind them. They are not graven images which we adore, but simply human creations which, however artistic and beautiful, only suggest in limited fashion the realities behind them.

Jesus Christ

Jesus Christ is, of course, the ultimate sign or symbol. Both human and divine, this Son of God and yet son of Mary reveals to us in a visible, although mysterious manner, that is, never fully to be grasped, who God is. In Catholic teaching, Jesus is the Eternal Word in heaven coming down on earth in human form and living among us. People saw him born, lived with him as he grew, marveled at his remarkable teaching, observed his miraculous deeds, watched him suffer, saw him die, and even experienced his risen presence three days after Good Friday.

They witnessed the visible human nature of Christ, but were invited to go beyond that in faith to recognize the invisible divine world from which he came. Thomas the Apostle, once doubting and now believing, expressed this move from the human to the divine, from the visible to the invisible with his classic affirmation of faith: "My Lord and my God" (John 20:28).

The interior of Catholic churches, therefore, quite naturally features many images or representations of Jesus and his life on earth as well as conceptions of Christ's existence in heaven.

The crucifix with its image of Jesus fixed to the cross recalls his suffering on Good Friday. Since we never stop at Calvary, but always move on three days to the resurrection, some churches have a crucifix with attached symbols of victory and triumph also. Our own processional crucifix, for example, has three sparkling glass crystals at each of the cross's four end points.

The stations of the cross are an artist's conception of the Savior on his sorrowful journey from being condemned by Pilate to his burial in the tomb.

In the apse of our cathedral, large stained glass windows picture the birth of Jesus, his death on the cross, his resurrection, and his ascension into heaven together with the Holy Spirit's descent upon those gathered in the Upper Room at Pentecost.

As we have noted, the rose window at the front entrance portrays Christ in heaven, wearing a crown as king of kings and placing a crown upon his mother Mary's head, designating her as Queen of the Universe.

Mary, the Mother of Jesus

Almost all, if not every Catholic church will include within it a representation of Mary, the mother of Jesus. This usually will be a statue, sometimes with the Christ child in her arms. The representation may in addition, however, take the form of a mural or a stained glass window. These feature the Madonna alone or with her son during one or another of the episodes in their lives

This statue above a side altar depicts the Holy Family—Jesus as a young child with Mary, his mother, and Joseph, her husband.

together, such as the birth at Bethlehem, the adolescent child lost and found in the temple, or at the foot of the cross.

One of our side altars contains a statue of the Holy Family, Mary, Joseph, and the child Jesus.

Murals along the two sides of the nave in our cathedral reflect invocations contained in the Litany of Loretto, a series of titles honoring Mary that dates back to the twelfth century. The titles appear above an angel holding a shield which symbolizes the invocation. For example:

> Queen of peace—a dove with a twig in its mouth recalling the story of Noah, the ark, and the dove returning with a "plucked off olive leaf" in its bill (Genesis 8:11)
> Mirror of justice—a scale with two suspended weight plates
> Queen of martyrs—a sword with two palm leaves of victory
> Mother of Christ—a large M with the chi-rho symbol of Christ
> Queen of prophets—an open scroll

Some grow uncomfortable with the Catholic emphasis on Mary, even complaining that this woman is given more honor than Jesus, that she is raised to a divine level, that Catholicism promotes worship of Christ's mother.

An analogy might help with this concern. In most families, when people praise the children, that pleases their mother; when people honor a mother, that pleases her children. It would seem, as a parallel, that worshiping Christ, her son, pleases Mary, the mother of Jesus, and honoring his mother pleases her divine son.

While Roman Catholics honor Mary in special ways, the Church clearly teaches that, while blessed uniquely by God, she is a creature, not the Creator, human, not divine, worthy of our admiration and honor, but not a suitable recipient of the adoration and worship due to God alone.

The Catholic Church declares that this Jewish maiden was singularly graced by God. It maintains that Mary was conceived without sin, a virgin before, during, and after the birth of Christ, the mother of Jesus Christ, the Son of God, and therefore the mother of God, sinless during her life, taken up into heaven after her days on earth and reigning now as queen of heaven and earth.

Those beliefs translate into words, services, and objects honoring Mary, the mother of Jesus, which may make some uncomfortable. Flowery words about the Virgin elevate her almost to the divine. May crownings, novenas in her name, and processions at shrines such as Lourdes in France may seem like an exaggeration which downplays her son. Statues and images of Mary with and without her child appear in churches, on the dashboard of automobiles, and on the lawn at homes of committed Catholics.

Such devotional words, services, and objects, however, reflect only a recognition of the many gifts with which Mary has been blessed by God, not the adoration of a divine being. Catholics may say they are praying to Mary when they really mean that their prayers are through the mother to the son. We can return to the analogy of the human relationship between mother and children. We may ask a mother's intervention with one of her offspring or vice versa.

The words used in Catholic prayers reinforce that distinction between the Creator and creature. We ask Mary to intercede on our behalf, to pray for us, or to speak to her son about us.

The Litany of Loretto, cited earlier, mirrors that distinction between adoration of God and petitions to Mary. It begins with invocations to the Father, Son, and Holy Spirit. The response to those invocations is, "Have mercy on us." The subsequent invocations honoring Mary such as Mother of Christ, Refuge of Sinners, and Queen of All Saints is, on the other hand, "Pray for us." The difference between those two responses clearly distinguishes the human, but richly blessed, Mary from the divine, transcendent, and adorable God.

Other Saints

Saints are persons who lived holy lives on earth and are now with God in heaven. These were not perfect people, but individuals who strove mightily to walk in God's ways, never giving up, and always starting over when they failed. Some have been recognized or canonized by the Church, declared to be now with the Lord in heaven, because of miracles worked here on earth through their intercession. Countless others are certainly there, but not officially and individually recognized by the Church. The liturgical year celebrates these numberless "unofficial" or anonymous saints on All Saints Day, November 1.

Most churches will have at least one or several images of saints in addition to the representation of Mary. Those will usually be canonized individuals with some kind of connection or bonding to the people of the parish.

Our cathedral has several dozen persons represented on stained glass windows high up on the two side walls of the nave. There are "contemporary saints," as opposed to the apostles and older saints such as St. Augustine and St. Jerome. These modern models include people such as Saints Francis and Clare, Benedict and Scholastica, Dominic and Catherine of Siena, even though they all lived many centuries before the cathedral was constructed from 1870 to 1910.

Newer churches and some older ones today often feature images of relatively new saints. They reflect the contemporary trend in the Church to canonize a greater variety of saints—from different countries and cultures, from diverse backgrounds and disparate time periods, some within the past century.

As we mentioned at the beginning of the book, St. Patrick's Cathedral in New York City, old and majestic in itself, has added along the side aisles shrines honoring a diversity of saints, some of whom recent popes have canonized. The Cathedral of Our Lady of Angels in Los Angeles, California, consecrated in 2002, likewise has areas dedicated to saints of diverse ethnic origin who lived in different eras of the Church's history.

Devotional Candles

Lighting candles in connection with personal prayer has long been a strong part of Catholic devotional life, that is, a religious action permitted, but not required, by the Church.

A shrine with its distinctive sculpture of Mary as an older, caring woman contains devotional candles lit by the many visitors who stop here to pray for themselves and for others.

The candle stands are normally located near some statue or image of a saint or of Christ himself. People stop before the shrine, drop a coin or a bill in the secure receptacle provided, light a candle, and then pray for the intention in their mind or upon their heart. In doing so they honor the person represented and ask that their prayer continue after they leave the church.

About five hundred persons each week stop at our cathedral's Marian shrine, the converted baptistry, which provides two kinds of these votive candles. The visitors make an offering or donation, light the five-hour- or fifty-hour-size candle, then kneel or sit down for a few moments to whisper in their hearts petitions for people and needs close to them.

The popularity of this form of devotion has waned during the past decades for various reasons. The risk of fire and the consequent pressure from insurance companies is one. The burden of maintenance is another. The objection from some that lighting a votive candle is an almost superstitious carry-over from medieval days is still a third reason, and probably the most significant factor causing a decline. Substituting electric votive lights eliminates the first two difficulties, although many regret the loss of an option to light a real candle that actually burns.

Those several hundred who light candles weekly at our church would resent being told that this devotional practice is superstitious, out of date, and contrary to Church teaching. These visitors include a former college and NFL football coach, a lawyer and her husband who always stop at the shrine following Sunday Mass, a most successful businessman who with his wife also lights a candle after the Eucharist, a bright, sophisticated and searching young executive who derives spiritual comfort and guidance at Our Lady's shrine through frequent trips there from his nearby office building.

The famous grotto at the University of Notre Dame with its enormous number of burning votive candles exemplifies this still popular devotion, quite important to some people.

The flame flickering for five hours to five days symbolizes the person's prayer continuing on long after the individual has departed and resumed work or other activities.

Liturgical Colors

As a particular way of symbolizing events in the year, churches generally use different colors for the vestments and altar decorations. Purple indicates a time of expectation, purification, or penance. White or gold expresses joy and triumph. Red is a sign of royalty, fire, and martyrdom; green, of life and growth. The following simplified table of season and feasts in the Church year may help clarify this use of liturgical colors:

Season or Feast	Time and Meaning	Liturgical Color
Advent	four weeks of preparation for Christ's coming on December 25	purple
Christmas-Epiphany	Christ's birth and early manifestation	white
Lent	forty days of penitential preparation for baptism and Easter	purple
Easter	Christ's resurrection and the risen Lord's appearance to his followers	white
Pentecost	descent of the Holy Spirit (Acts 2)	red
Ordinary Time	the Church hearing and living Jesus' message	green

Crosses and crucifixes, statues and stained glass windows, burning votive candles and vestments of different colors—all these and the other symbols inside Catholic churches—have a single function or goal. They are meant to lead us through the visible to the invisible, from the here to the hereafter, from the things of earth to the joys of heaven, from time to eternity, from the mundane to the transcendent, from the material to the spiritual. In brief, these symbols possess both the purpose and the power to help us experience on a frequent basis the peace-giving presence of our awesome God.

Heroes and Heroines, Models and Helpers

The United States Connection

At St. Patrick's Cathedral in New York City, midway down the right side aisle, directly across from the contemporary shrine honoring St. John Neumann, is an equally bright and modern alcove dedicated to St. Elizabeth Ann Bayley Seton (1774-1821). Elizabeth Bayley was born into an Episcopalian family and absorbed from her family good habits of prayer, love for the sacred scriptures, the practice of nightly examining her conscience and concern for those in need.

At the age of nineteen, this high-spirited young lady, considered at that time the belle of New York City society, married William Magee Seton, a wealthy merchant. Within a decade they had five children, but then her husband's business and health failed. They traveled to Italy seeking recovery of his health; instead he died in Elizabeth's arms leaving her, at thirty, a penniless widow with five small children to support.

During her time in Italy she became attracted to the Roman Catholic Church because of its emphasis on the Real Presence, devotions in honor of Mary, and traditions dating back to the apostles and to Christ.

Upon her return to New York City, Elizabeth Bayley Seton became a Catholic at St. Peter's Church in lower Manhattan, the parish closest to the "ground zero" area of the terrorists attacks on September 11, 2001.

Most of her family and friends rejected Mrs. Seton because of this conversion to Catholicism. However, a sympathetic person invited her to open a school for girls in Baltimore. She did so in 1808, thus establishing the nation's first parochial school. Her work in education spread, and she also founded a number of orphanages.

A group of women gathered around Mother Seton, drawn by her personal holiness and intense dedication to helping at-risk children. They eventually formed the first American religious community, the Sisters of Charity, based on the rule of life developed by St. Vincent de Paul.

In addition to the hardships in her life sketched above, St. Elizabeth Ann Seton also suffered the early death of her mother, a baby sister, and two young daughters, as well as the constant anxiety caused by a wayward son. Yet in the midst of all these burdens she maintained a cheerful and hope-filled attitude. The secret to that joyful serenity were her two great devotions: complete abandonment to the will of God and a deep love for the Blessed Sacrament.

Mother Seton once wrote: "God has given me a great deal to do, and I have always and hope always to prefer his will to every wish of my own."

St. Elizabeth Ann reiterated this thought in advice for the sisters of her newly established community: "The first end I propose in our daily work is to do the will of God; secondly, to do it in the manner he wills it; and thirdly, to do it because it is his will." The office of readings in the Liturgy of the Hours for her feast on January 4 contains those words.

Mother Seton was buried in Emmitsburg, Maryland, and in 1975 became the first American-born citizen to be declared a saint.

Our Lady of Angels Cathedral in Los Angeles, as we would expect, contains among its tapestries of 133 heroes and heroines, models and helpers, a representation of St. Elizabeth Ann Bayley Seton. Her life explains why the shrine in New York City portrays Mother Seton with a book in her hand and child before her.

Beyond the Church

At the end of every Mass, the priest or deacon dismisses the gathered community with a charge or mission. The sacramentary provides several formulas for that dismissal, including this one, "Go in peace to love and serve the Lord."

Having heard God's Word and received Christ's Body and Blood, those at that eucharistic celebration leave the church with renewed wisdom and guidance, strength and courage. The task now is to build up the Church and make this a better world.

Familiar biblical words render that challenge more specific. Matthew's description about the judgment of the nations can make us uncomfortable with our inadequate responses to Jesus' words about his being hungry, thirsty, a stranger, naked, ill, or in prison. Whatever we did or failed to do to one of these least of Christ's brothers or sisters, the Lord warns, we did or failed to do to him. Few, if any, human beings perfectly fulfill that command (Matthew 25:31-46).

The letter of James provides a similar stern warning about the responsibility of Christians toward those who are in any need.

> If a brother or sister has nothing to wear and has no food for the day, and one of you says to them, "Go in peace, keep warm, and eat well," but you do not give them the necessities of body, what good is it? So also faith of itself, if it does not have works, is dead. (James 2:15-17)

It is safe to maintain that every Catholic church in the United States contains many of the inspiring symbols described in this book. But each parish also provides some structured opportunities for its members upon leaving the sacred space inside to fulfill this charge to serve the Lord outside the church walls. There will be many more options in certain parishes than in others, but all share the identical goal of loving God through service of neighbor. This usually begins with personal invitations to volunteer for particular tasks or general requests to offer one's time and talent for a variety of parish programs. This latter event ordinarily occurs on a weekend at Masses in the Spring or Fall. Called by such titles as Volunteer, Time-and-Talent, or Stewardship weekends, the procedure may involve, for example, a sign-up form, testimonies of volunteers at Mass, or a time-and-talent fair featuring booths describing major opportunities for service.

One parish developed a 2002-2003 volunteer form that offered over fifty possibilities for parishioners—from altar servers (fourth grade and up) to golden-age club members.

Our cathedral has a strong commitment to the homeless, poor, and the elderly, and ministers to them. As illustrations of that service we participate in an ecumenical Samaritan Center, which serves several hundred hungry people in need of a full meal each afternoon; we offer a nutritious and hot breakfast every Wednesday morning for one hundred homeless men; we support a Downtown Emergency Assistance Service Center, which provides from the food pantry essential provisions for four hundred to five hundred households; we host a Catholic school which creates a safe, loving, and quality education for one hundred at-risk boys and girls who are mostly African American, not Catholic, and from below poverty-level-income homes; we train and coordinate dozens of men and women to visit the sick and homebound; we collect once a month at all the Masses a huge quantity of canned and boxed goods for the D.E.A.S. food pantry, items brought to Masses by parishioners and transported across the street to the center after the Eucharist; we facilitate sixty adults who mentor on an individual basis children at the school, spending one hour each week with the same boy or girl for an entire year.

In addition to such extensive and impressive efforts for those in need, our cathedral has the usual large corps of volunteers who serve at worship (e.g., readers, eucharistic ministers, musicians), engage in youth ministry, take part in religious education (e.g., teachers, RCIA team members, marriage preparation guides) and perform many necessary administrative tasks.

These examples are replicated in more than eighteen thousand Catholic parishes throughout the country with varying emphases and to an even more ambitious degree. The pattern or ideal for all these parishes is identical. People enter the church from their busy and sometimes burdensome worlds. They proceed to a serene and sacred space which through its silence and symbols gradually lifts up their spirits and draws their attention to God on high. In this holy place they hear holy words, receive the eucharistic Holy One, and encounter the holy through other rituals and personal prayer. Then, restored, refreshed, and renewed, they depart from the church and return to their worlds, confident that these experiences of the divine will make a difference in their own lives and through them in the lives of others.

Acknowledgments

This book would not have become a reality without Michael Leach, the publisher of Orbis Books at Maryknoll. For more than a decade, Mike has been for me a fine editor, enthusiastic supporter and very good friend. After hearing of the need for a volume like this, he judged that I would be the suitable person to write it. For Michael's encouragement and guidance over these ten plus years, I am deeply grateful.

Several resources were most helpful in the writing.

Robert Barron's *Heaven in Stone and Glass: Experiencing the Spirituality of the Great Cathedrals* (New York: Crossroad, 2000) enabled me to look at our own Cathedral from a deeper and richer perspective.

Judith Ann Kollar, with her book *A User-Friendly Parish: Becoming a More Welcoming Community* (Mystic, Conn: Twenty-Third Publications, 1998), helped set the welcoming tone of chapter 1.

Two books provided details about the saints featured in the "Heroes and Heroines, Models and Helpers" section at the end of each chapter. Franciscans Leonard Foley and Pat McCloskey combined to produce the fourth revised edition of *Saint of the Day: Lives, Lessons and Feasts* (St. Anthony Messenger Press, 2001). Enzo Lodi prepared *Saints of the Roman Calendar*, with translation and adaptation by Jordan Anmann, O.P. (Staten Island, N.Y.: Alba House, 1992).

Two articles in *Saint Anthony Messenger* gave additional details about St. Juan Diego and St. Elizabeth Ann Seton (Judy Ball, "Pioneer Saint of a Young Nation" [January 2003], and Virgilio P. Elizondo, "St. Juan Diego: New World Apostle" [July 2002]).

Excerpts from four of my earlier publications appear in this book: chapter 1, *The Mystery and the Meaning of the Mass* (New York: Crossroad, 1999); chapter 7, *Stations of the Cross with Pope John Paul II* (Liguori, Mo.: Liguori, 1994), and *Together in Peace* (Notre Dame, Ind.: Ave Maria Press, 1975); chapter 9, *What It Means to Be Catholic* (Los Angeles: Franciscan Communications, 1986).

Edward J. Long, a cathedral parishioner and professional photographer, provided the illustrations, which should make the content of this book clearer, especially for a reader not familiar with the inside of a Catholic church.

Various staff people both at St. Patrick's Cathedral and the Cathedral of Our Lady of the Angels in Los Angeles were most gracious, prompt, and efficient in supplying the photographs of those two impressive and distinct structures. In particular, I extend my deep gratitude to Robert Shea at St. Patrick's and Hans Daklia at Our Lady of the Angels for specific assistance.

I wish to thank Monsignor Donald Krebs for his tour of those churches in Fargo, North Dakota, and Moorhead, Minnesota. Moreover, Monsignor Kevin Kostelnik, Rector of Our Lady of Angels Cathedral in Los Angeles, likewise extended gracious hospitality to me, along with his detailed explanations as we walked through the entire church complex.

Art and Patricia Gale collaborated once again as they have for nearly three decades in transferring my handwritten manuscript to the computer and ultimately the final version to the necessary disk.

I am most grateful also to Bishop Thomas Costello, Auxiliary Bishop of Syracuse as well as my friend and colleague for over fifty years, who very, very carefully read through the manuscript with his keen editorial and theological skills.

May the Lord richly bless those who aided in the creation of this book and all who will read it.